un‸common
courtesy

❖❖❖❖❖❖❖❖❖❖❖❖❖❖❖❖❖❖❖❖❖✖❖❖❖❖❖❖❖❖❖❖❖❖❖❖❖❖❖❖❖❖❖

un^common courtesy

The Basics of
Good Behavior
FOR A BADLY BEHAVED WORLD

JENNIFER M. WOOD

Avon, Massachusetts

Copyright © 2011 by F+W Media, Inc.
All rights reserved.
This book, or parts thereof, may not be reproduced in any
form without permission from the publisher; exceptions are
made for brief excerpts used in published reviews.

Published by
Adams Media, a division of F+W Media, Inc.
57 Littlefield Street, Avon, MA 02322. U.S.A.
www.adamsmedia.com

Contains material adapted and abridged from *The Everything® Etiquette Book*,
2nd Edition, by Leah Ingram, copyright © 2005 by F+W Media, Inc., ISBN 10:
1-59337-383-X, ISBN 13: 978-1-59337-383-2.

ISBN 10: 1-4405-1203-5
ISBN 13: 978-1-4405-1203-2
eISBN 10: 1-4405-2655-9
eISBN 13: 978-1-4405-2655-8

Printed in the United States of America.

10 9 8 7 6 5 4 3 2 1

Library of Congress Cataloging-in-Publication Data
is available from the publisher.

This publication is designed to provide accurate and authoritative information
with regard to the subject matter covered. It is sold with the understanding that
the publisher is not engaged in rendering legal, accounting, or other professional
advice. If legal advice or other expert assistance is required, the services of a com-
petent professional person should be sought.
—From a *Declaration of Principles* jointly adopted by a Committee of the
American Bar Association and a Committee of Publishers and Associations

Many of the designations used by manufacturers and sellers to distinguish their
product are claimed as trademarks. Where those designations appear in this book
and Adams Media was aware of a trademark claim, the designations have been
printed with initial capital letters.

This book is available at quantity discounts for bulk purchases.
For information, please call 1-800-289-0963.

Dedication

To my parents, Dennis and Jacqueline—one of whom consistently set an example for the "wrong" way to conduct yourself in any given situation, while the other was always (fortunately) there to correct the behavior. (I'm not saying who did which.) And to my husband, Jamie, who permanently quieted my mother's etiquette lessons that began with the phrase, "You'll never get a fella if . . ."

Table of Contents

Acknowledgments

Though I've never used the term "etiquette expert" to define myself, I have often voiced (threatened, really) the desire to send a handwritten note to every badly behaved person I've encountered with a short lesson on just how far good manners can take you. Thanks to the team at Adams for making this happen, especially Michelle Roy Kelly, for understanding my deep desire to rid the world of loutish behavior and recommending me for the project accordingly.

Thanks also to Wendy Simard for elevating my text with her editorial expertise. And to the ever-supportive Brendan O'Neill, who has been an amazing source of encouragement and positive energy from first pitch to final edit.

Finally, I'd like to thank the many, many people— friends, family members, foes, complete strangers—who have served as examples of behaviors both bad and good throughout this book (whether they know it or not).

Introduction

Whether we care to admit it or not, we've all been perpetrators of crimes against good behavior at least once in our lives (okay, *maybe* twice). You've snuck a last-minute candy bar into your preexisting pile of a dozen items at the 12-items-or-less checkout or pretended not to notice that annoying acquaintance from your child's school when you walked past her on the street . . . even after she has called your name at the top of her lungs. Perhaps you've pulled the "I've got another call coming in that I have to take" fakeout when you can't seem to shake your chatterbox friend from the line, or have hit the gas pedal just a little harder than usual to acquire that primo parking space a few steps from the mall entrance, despite the farther-away car that was waiting for the same spot . . . and clearly there first.

Hey, nobody's perfect. Not even the most well-mannered individual can bite his or her tongue *all* the time. The truth is that common courtesy is not so common after all.

This book likely landed in your hot little hands in one of two ways: you purchased it for yourself as a proactive measure to discover the small things you can do to get ahead in life, both personally and professionally. Or it was presented to you by someone else, friend or foe, who (on some level) believes that you could use a brief refresher on the dos and don'ts of civilized living. (Yes, even if she *did* call it a "gag gift.")

In either case, congratulations! Whether you asked for it or it was forced upon you, there's no shame in wanting to brush up on your behavior. But etiquette isn't skin deep. It's not something you switch on in public and kick off with your shoes when you get home at night. Manners are a way of life—a religion of sorts—that need to be ingrained and come naturally in order to be genuine.

With today's glut of handheld electronics—cell phones, e-readers, iPads, etc.—we are moving further and further away from our polite roots. Today's youth culture seems unable to communicate in full sentences and thinks emoticons are a standard form of punctuation. Which means that the time to reverse the trend is *now*. With this book as your guide, you can lead a revolution to prove that chivalry is not dead. If acid-washed jeans can make a comeback, so can common courtesy.

Fifteen Ways to Better Manners

As extensive as this book is—with common rules for basic etiquette at home, in the workplace, on vacation, and just about any other location you might find yourself—there are bound to be exceptional circumstances you'll face on occasion that aren't covered here. Even if there is no specific entry for your particular scenario within these pages, here are fifteen ground rules that can help you be the perfect guest/host/employee/spouse/sibling/child/student/what-have-you in just about any situation. As most of them are clichés, they shouldn't be too hard to remember, either.

1. **Say "please," "thank you," and "you're welcome."** Okay, so this one is sort of a gimme, as it's (hopefully) a lesson mom and dad taught you shortly after you began uttering "mama" and "dada." But these three simple phrases—"please," "thank you," "you're welcome"—are the foundation of polite behavior.

2. **Think before you speak.** If you reflect back on some of the most regrettable things you've ever said or done in your life, they probably occurred in the heat of the moment—an angry word exchanged with your spouse that you still wish you hadn't said, a biting retort to a question that you completely misinterpreted. Never let your emotions control your mouth.

3. **Patience is a virtue.** This rule could also be called "Good things come to those who wait." Whether in your car or at the store, always wait your turn. Never cut in front of a line or pretend you don't see that winding line of people, simply because you believe that your transaction will "only take a second." It's self-centered and just plain rude. Yes, even if you're just getting the newspaper in a sea of office drones custom-ordering their favorite caffeinated concoctions. Buy a subscription, buddy.

4. **Don't speak out of turn.** When you have a point to make, you have the right to expect that the opposing party is going to hear you out completely—without

interruption. Never take that right away from some-one else by inserting your comments into the middle of his or her train of thought. Even if you're *positive* the world isn't flat.

5. **Just say no.** Politeness doesn't mean that you always have to be agreeable. It's about being honest and thinking of other people's feelings, but never doing something you don't want to just because someone asks. While the word "no" has an ostensibly negative connotation, there are plenty of ways to make declin-ing an offer a totally positive experience.

6. **Stay in the positive.** There's always a way to end a con-versation on a positive note, even when you're telling someone no. "No, but I really appreciate the offer" or "I can't, but thanks for thinking of me" are just two ways to put a positive spin on a rejection. If you're turning someone down and know that you'll never accept their invitation in the future (an unwanted suitor, perhaps), don't drag out the process with "I'm busy that night, but perhaps we could do it another time" if you don't mean it. It will only mean repeat-ing the exercise until you eventually hurt the person when he finally understands your lack of intention of ever getting together. The same goes for those times when you're forced to give someone your constructive criticism; always be sure to point out the positives, too (and put those out there first).

7. **Watch the potty mouth.** Few things scream "poor character" more loudly to an outside observer than

a vocabulary marked with f-bombs and other four-letter words. Sometimes you can't help but express yourself with expletives, but "fudge" and "cheese and crackers" in lieu of their R-rated alternatives are bound to offend far fewer people (and make a few others giggle).

8. **Lend a helping hand.** Wherever you are, find a way to be helpful. Whether it's carrying some presentation materials for your coworker, holding the door open for a stranger, or offering to clean dishes for your dinner host, everyone appreciates a helping hand. And even those who don't take you up on the offer will remember the sentiment. (Hey, some of us just prefer the way we wash our own dishes.)

9. **Keep your mouth shut.** Yes, you and your BFF are going to gossip about your circle of friends from time to time. And you and your spouse might want to dish about the marital problems your next-door neighbors may or may not be having. But when you're in mixed company—particularly if there's even one person you don't know very well—save your judgments. Being critical of others only makes you look bad, so don't speak ill of others. Even if they totally deserve it.

10. **Do unto others as you would have them do unto you.** Before you take any action against another person—whether it's declining an invitation or responding to an upsetting e-mail—play out in your head the scenario of what might likely happen as a result of your response. Think of how you would feel if you were

being told the same thing and, if there's a chance of offense or misinterpretation, tweak your response accordingly.

11. **Follow the rules.** If a sign tells you to turn your cell phone off, do it. If someone asks that you take your shoes off upon entering their home, abide by the house rules. Good manners come from honoring a request, not questioning why it was made in the first place.

12. **Teach your children well.** Good manners are contagious and easy to spread to those around you—especially your children. Reinforcing the importance of good manners from the time a child begins to speak will ensure that politeness is one trait that your offspring will pass on to their own kids. If only there were a gene for that!

13. **Give people the benefit of the doubt.** We all make mistakes. And we all deserve to be forgiven for a momentary lapse in judgment or good manners. So give people the benefit of the doubt and be quick to forgive. Until it happens a second time.

14. **Be full of compliments.** But only if you mean them. Using the same tired line again and again will land you in trouble when you've already told every woman in the office how nicely her lipstick complements her eyes.

15. **Get to know the words "I'm sorry."** Apologizing doesn't make you look weak—it makes you seem human. We all make mistakes. Be honest enough to admit when

you've made one. Even if it seems like you're apologizing for something once a day. And if you *do* find yourself apologizing for the same thing again and again, find a way to stop the offending action. There's a limit to how many times a person will accept an apology for the same infraction.

CHAPTER 1

At Home

❖❖❖❖❖❖❖❖❖❖❖❖❖❖❖❖❖❖❖✠❖❖❖❖❖❖❖❖❖❖❖❖❖❖❖❖❖❖❖

Ahhh, home. The one place where you can truly be yourself—where you can lounge around in pajamas all day, turn a bowl of ice cream into three square meals, and use your treadmill as an ersatz hamper if you feel so inclined.

All that may be true, but good manners start at home—yes, even when no one is watching. If you're serious about living a well-mannered life, it needs to become a natural reflex, not a put-on social grace you turn on and off when the mood strikes you.

Home may be your sanctuary, but there are plenty of ways your patience can be tried under your very own roof. From nosy neighbors to noisy pets, if charity begins at home, then so does etiquette.

Welcome Home!

Whether it's a grand old Victorian or a 123-square-foot studio apartment, moving into a new place of residence (new to you, at least) is an exciting prospect, and a cause worth celebrating with friends and family. Do it with a housewarming party.

> It doesn't matter if you choose to host your own party or you have a friend who wants to do it for you, never forget the purpose of the fete: to welcome guests into your new home. **While a 100-car garage may be part of the home's amenities, this is not the time to boast about how your classic car collection is rivaled only by Jay Leno's (the time to do that is when Leno invites you onto his show).** Nor is it an opportunity to ask your friends and family to gift you with all the kitchen gadgets you can't afford to buy yourself. It's not okay to host a party for fifty if you don't have the plates and forks with which to serve them. If you're living in a work in progress, wait until the masterpiece is complete.

You can call it a "painting party" if you want, but events where guests are expected to get their hands (and feet) dirty need to be spelled out in advance. So be up-front about it from the get-go. No one wants to be lured into free manual labor on the promise of pizza and beer. Well, some people do; let *them* be the ones to help you.

> If you're the guest instead of the host, you should never arrive at a housewarming party empty-handed. The nice thing about this type of event is that a new home is somewhat of a blank slate, so there is a plethora of affordable, totally appropriate gifts from which to choose. A bottle of wine, a fancy candle, a dozen tulips, a gift certificate to a home improvement store, or a set of cookie trays with a few of your favorite recipes are all great ways to make

someone feel at home in his or her new pad. Just be careful not to infuse *too* much of your personal style into a decorative gift. **A six-foot, neon-green vase may work with your interior-decor, but it won't meld as well with the homeowner's penchant for French country-style roosters.**

> By the same token, a gift of a home-cooked dish to share with your host and your fellow guests may seem like a thoughtful idea (and it is, truly), but it's always best to check with your host ahead of time when it comes to adding something to the menu. Your kids may consider your gumbo world-class, but your host may not want to give your spicy, down-home treat a place at the table. Especially when her menu calls for sushi.

Like a Good Neighbor

Unless you reside on your very own private island (in which case you've really got no one to impress but yourself), you're going to have to deal with neighbors. Good ones, bad ones, nosy ones, noisy ones—neighbors come in every shape, size, and degree of tolerability. The best way to get along with those folks who share a property line is to heed the old adage "Treat others as you would like to be treated." Strike the right balance of friendliness and privacy and a neighborhood can be a wonderful thing.

> Whether it's with an enthusiastic "Hello!" or a friendly wave in their direction, always acknowledge your neighbors

when you see them—even if you always seem to be coming and going at the same time. There's no need to have a full-on conversation every time you see each other, but a without-fail greeting is enough to keep you on their good side. And score you an invite to this year's block party.

> If you're new to a neighborhood, introduce yourself to everyone you meet and ask the other person's name so that you can greet them with it in the future. "Top of the morning, Ted!" Nothing makes someone feel more important than being remembered. If, on the other hand, you're the neighborhood veteran, deem yourself the community welcome wagon. **When someone new moves into the 'hood, make like a Norman Rockwell painting and welcome them to the area.** Embrace your insider status: stop by, introduce yourself, and offer up some suggestions on where to get the best pint of Guinness or the freshest kumquats.

> Get to know your neighbors when you can—find out who they are, what they do, who they reside with, etc. It's great to be able to call the people who live around you "friends." And even greater when you can call on them to water your plants—or your cat—if you're going to be out of town for a few days.

> If you like your community cohorts enough—and feel so inclined—host a casual get-together of local folks on occasion. It could be a simple, happy-hour kind of event—everyone brings a bottle of wine and you provide the cheese

and crackers—or a summer afternoon cookout with all the kids in tow. **A happy hood turns your domestic domicile into the haven you've always dreamed it could be.**

Thin Walls

If your living situation calls for any sort of shared wall—be it an apartment, condo, or townhouse—you're going to get an inside peek (or listen) into what *really* goes on in your neighbors' homes on occasion. Whether they know it or not.

> The golden rule of shared-wall living is to be conscious—and cautious—of how much noise you are generating. Any noise-making devices—televisions, stereos, pets, humans—should be set at a volume appropriate for your ears only. **Your favorite reality show will be just as melodramatic at a nondeafening sound level.**

But never forget that it's not just the walls through which sound travels, it's the floors and ceilings, too. If you have a dog who loves to run the length of the house on a loop or kids who are practicing to be in the WWE, do what you can to relegate that rough-housing to a specific, more soundproofed area (say, that one couch with the seriously fluffy cushions) or better yet *outside.*

> Like the '80s song told us: voices carry. Sometimes louder than you think. You wouldn't stage a disagreement with your spouse on the front lawn as your own version of community theater, so keep your voices down and your wits about you at all times, even in the heat of battle. The same thing goes for moments of intimacy. **Think of your neighbors as friends in the next room—make love and war accordingly.**

> One of the great pleasures of having a place to call your own is to show it off. Parties can be a lot of fun for you, but a nightmare for your neighbors if the noise level gets out of control and lasts all night. The best way to deal with the problem: invite your neighbors! It will make them less likely to call the cops when that one inebriated party guest mistakes your front lawn for the restroom.

Apartment Dwelling

It's easy to get swept up in the excitement of apartment hunting, but if you think about the practicalities of living in a space before you sign on the dotted line, you can save yourself a lot of headaches (literal and figurative) in the future. **If there's a nightclub outside your window, decide now whether you want to become the person who screams "Keep it down out there!" at 4 A.M. each morning when the revelry spills outside.** (And what well-mannered person would do *that*? A sleep-deprived one, maybe.)

> One of the most awkward parts of apartment living is dealing with conflict. Disagreements are a part of life and can occur with a parent, child, spouse, or complete stranger. The easiest way to squash a conflict is to address it head-on, quickly and with total honesty—and to offer a solution if you have one. **If you work from home and your neighbor's dog barks from 9 to 5, why not offer to play the role of dog-walker once a day?** Picking up after a pooch that isn't yours may not be the ideal way to spend your lunch break, but if it helps to curb the pup's anxiety—and vocalizing—isn't that worth it?

> If the thought of engaging in a neighborly tête-à-tête causes you to break out into a full-bodied sweat, contact your landlord instead of penning an anonymous letter (which is never a good idea). It's part of his job to deal with issues swiftly and discreetly. But don't be surprised if the neighbor suspects you. (He's noisy, not dumb.)

> Sometimes the architectural details of a building are as much to blame for excessive noise as those seemingly hard-of-hearing neighbors. There are things that you can do to help the situation once you've identified where the noise is coming from (meaning a wall, floor or ceiling). Tapestries and other thick wall hangings may seem a little strange nailed across the ceiling, but if it muffles your upstairs neighbor's penchant for watching *Glee* at top volume, so be it. Rugs on the floor will help insulate against noise filtering up from downstairs, as well as muffle whatever sounds you're making in your own apartment. Bulky

furniture can help reduce the noise that travels from your own apartment, too—so now that oversized chair you've been eyeing can serve *two* purposes.

Odors can result from many causes—idle trash cans, overzealous cooking, etc. If you happen to have overcooked something and see (and smell) that the smoke is filling up the hallways, open all the windows and doors you can to move the smell from indoors to out as quickly as possible. If your grandmother's famous fennel turkey recipe tastes like heaven but smells like hell, save it for your first night as a *homeowner*.

> Balconies, patios, porches, and backyards are a great apartment amenity, but become less desirable when shared with a neighbor. Make sure to draw an invisible line between your possessions and theirs, and never use something that doesn't belong to you without asking permission first—even if you're almost *positive* they've gone away for the weekend.

> If you're a smoker and want to use shared outdoor space to light up, discuss it with your neighbors first to identify a designated smoking area. People are much less likely to get angry or complain when you've asked their permission ahead of time. Ask first, *then* break out the cigars.

Common Area Common Sense

In any shared-wall living situation, there's going to be some other shared spaces—typically known as common areas—where it pays to pay extra-special attention to your behavior, lest you be labeled the local lout.

> The number one rule of traversing these common areas is to be mindful of the time and the amount of noise you are making. It's easy to forget how noise travels when you're stumbling in from an all-day pub crawl. But keep the recap of the day's event to yourself until you've reached your own apartment (and closed the door behind you).

Parking lots (or, in the case of homeowners, even garages and driveways) are another common area. If you have a car alarm, make sure it's an alarm of a more intelligent variety, meaning that it activates when someone is actually trying to boost your stereo, not when a wayward leaf finds its way onto your windshield.

> Outdoor space is a luxury, and often a common area in an apartment complex or condo community. If you or your kids are engaging in a personal activity on common ground—riding a bike, hosting a barbecue, etc.—be sure to tidy up after yourself as soon as you are finished. This is particularly important when it comes to walking your four-legged friends around the property (be it canine, feline, rodent, or otherwise). **No one likes the kind of surprise**

that a pampered pet leaves behind—particularly if it ends up on his or her favorite pair of shoes.

Home Ownership Has Its Privileges

Owning your own home: it's the American Dream, right? Don't let this dream turn into a nightmare by allowing—or contributing to—domestic delinquency in your neighborhood.

> In 1950s-era sitcoms, the neighborly "pop-in" was a charming diversion from one's housecleaning and other domestic drudgery. In today's faster-paced times, when our whereabouts at any time are just a Foursquare post away, that trend is reversing. Stopping by to borrow a cup of sugar is one thing; showing up unannounced with a glass of wine in one hand and a week's worth of gossip in your mouth is something else completely. **You may have a few hours to kill in the evening, but don't assume others share this luxury.** Before you know it, your neighbors will be pulling down their blinds and locking their doors at 5 P.M.—becoming prisoners in their own home so they don't have to listen to you rattle on about what sort of mischief your neighbors are getting up to.

Curb Appeal

Regardless of what exists behind the front door, a home's exterior projects a lot about its inhabitants. It's also the one part of a home that all neighbors and other passersby will see, so you will want to keep it neat and orderly. The only thing that neighbors should see on your lawn is grass and shrubbery. A broken-down car or old fridge is not a sight worth seeing. **You don't want to be the eyesore of the neighborhood—the house the neighborhood kids think is haunted.**

You've probably gazed at your neighbors' homes and thought about how you would decorate them differently if you lived there. Take that same judgmental eye to your own home on occasion and imagine how your neighbors might view your abode. Do you have spotlights that run all evening long, one of which shines directly into a neighbor's bedroom window? Is your bedazzling bright-pink front door the only thing folks in the neighborhood can talk about? Make sure there is no way your outdoor decor can impede on anyone else's property (or aesthetic values).

> At least once a week, of course, you'll need to air your garbage—on trash day. Don't just pile up your batch of garbage bags; maintain a selection of trash cans (with lids) and leave all trash within said cans on the sidewalk no earlier than the evening before they're scheduled to be picked up. In the morning, once the bags have been carted away, return the trash cans to their designated spot (the side of the house or garage, ideally). And don't forget that those

trash cans need to be cleaned out themselves from time to time, too.

> If you insist on showing your holiday spirit with a 20-foot inflatable Santa Claus, make sure the jolly guy isn't blocking other people's views, driveways, etc. Be aware that a garishly decorated home for the holidays is bound to stop traffic—*literally*. People driving by, especially those with tots in tow, will slow down to gaze and gawk. So shut that winter wonderland down no later than 9 P.M. If you're likely to forget to flip the power switch, put the entire display on a timer so that you're not the source of the neighborhood's collective insomnia.

> Even if you've been so busy reading this book that you haven't had a chance to read a paper or pay a bill in weeks, don't let them pile up outside your front door. If this is unavoidable because you're heading out of town for a few days, either ask a neighbor to help keep the outside of your home tidy by retrieving your newspapers and mail or call your delivery services and ask them to put a hold on all deliveries for as long as you are away. This will prevent eyesores and burglaries!

> Everyone appreciates a neighbor who maintains a fantastically landscaped lawn—but not if it means waking up to the sweet, sweet sounds of a lawn mower or leaf blower at the crack of dawn. **Save the yard work for the afternoon—at a time when anyone who is sleeping deserves to be woken up anyway.** The same goes

for construction projects: home improvements may help bolster property values in the neighborhood, but early-morning bulldozers will only leave your neighbors wishing you'd sell the place already so they can get some sleep.

> A sidewalk runs in front of your home, but it's public property. Treat it that way by making sure it's clear at all times. When inclement weather strikes, it's your responsibility to shovel it off. But don't just stop at the property lines; keep going if you've got the time—do your neighbors a small favor and get their walkways cleared. You'll be thankful when they return the favor next snowfall. Especially if it turns out to be a blizzard.

> If you have elderly or disabled neighbors, take it upon yourself to lend a helping hand—a hand with a shovel in it, that is—and clear their walkways, too. If you have kids, teach them the importance of helping out a neighbor in need and make it a family activity. You've found a great teachable moment and can pawn all of the *real* heavy lifting off on the youngsters.

Man's Best Friends

You may think your Pekingese's underbite is adorable, but not everyone appreciates a four-legged family member. Help keep the peace—and the dog catcher away—with a few easy rules when it comes to Fido, Kitty, and any other domesticated creature living under your roof.

> You adopted your pooch for a variety of reasons. Your neighbor did not. Don't force responsibility for Fido onto your neighbor by letting the dog roam through the neighborhood. First off, this is illegal in most places. Secondly, you have no idea of—or control over—what the little guy is getting up to when he's out of your sight and property lines. Keep all your pets in your very own backyard. This goes for Kitty, too, and just about any animal that can wander onto—or damage—a neighbor's property. And don't ever leave the house without a stockpile of plastic baggies to pick up after your dog. **Fido, and all of his bodily functions, are your responsibility, not the property owner whose lawn he favors.**

No one wants to visit a home where, upon walking through the door, he or she can tell just how many animals (and of which species) live there. Fur-covered furniture and pet-stained rugs speak more about you and your clandestine affair with squalor than your pet's housebreaking or shedding habits. Responsible pet ownership means additional house-cleaning, especially when you're expecting guests. There are plenty of products to help you rid your furniture and common areas of any evidence of pets. No one needs to walk in with black jeans and leave with calico ones.

> That little "arf" or "meow" sounds adorable to you, but no one wants to be awakened by the sound of a neighbor's menagerie of pets barking to get back into

the house or clawing their way through a screen door. Pet parenting is much like human parenting: you need to be aware of your little ones' whereabouts and safety at all times.

> You may be able to carry on an all-bark conversation with your dog, but don't force your neighbors to listen in on it. One or two barks to let you know that he's ready to come in is tolerable; anything that stretches into the 30 seconds or more category is infuriating. When in doubt, bring the pup inside.

> When you encounter another pet in your travels, always ask whether he or she is friendly before allowing your pets to interact. This goes for your two-legged pets, too (read: your kids). Teach your kids early and well that it's not okay to pet a strange animal. If Junior wants to be sure to emerge with both hands and all ten fingers intact, he must always ask the owner if it's okay first.

Personal Appearance

Maintaining one's personal appearance doesn't have to mean being camera-ready at all times—but it does help to be clean, well-groomed, and coifed whenever you leave the house. And it's essential to be appropriately dressed for whatever the occasion, even if that is a sweatpant-clad visit to the gym.

> While it's important to keep up with matters of personal cleanliness, good hygiene is not a spectator sport. **It's better that others** guess **that you brush your teeth regularly from your winning smile than know this from having you floss your teeth in their presence during a dinner party.**

> When it comes to alerting someone to an embarrassing oversight in personal appearance—be it a spot on her clothing or the soup du jour's garnish in her teeth, people seem to fall into one of two camps: those who tell and those who clam up. As embarrassing as it may be to the person with the offending faux pas to have it pointed out (even by a complete stranger), it will be much less upsetting if she knows it's been caught early on. She could spend a sleepless night recounting all the people she spoke to with that parsley leaf wedged between her front teeth.

Hand motions are an easy, effective, and completely polite way of alerting someone to an unsightly stain or something hanging from his nose. If someone emerges from the bathroom and is "flying low," i.e., his zipper is undone, let him know with a quick and to-the-point zip motion in your own nether regions.

> If someone has been kind enough to alert you to half a hamburger stuck in your teeth, don't stick your finger in your mouth and start poking around, flashing a big grin and asking "Did I get it?" every three seconds. Make your way to the bathroom—avoiding any chance for smiling or greeting others—and extricate that sucker in private. Try swishing a mouthful of water around and see if that does the trick.

CHAPTER 2

In the Workplace

Admit it: you've been known to let your manners slide a bit at home on occasion—to take a swig of milk directly from the carton or let the garbage can fill up to a state that just might put you on the health department's most wanted list. While we've all been known to get a little *too* comfortable when it comes to our personal domiciles, the workplace is one place where there's never an excuse for shoddy etiquette. It's also the one domain in which good manners can do more than just inspire envy in your not-so-civilized peers. Your decorous behavior can help you land that next great promotion or convince your boss to shell out generously come raise time. From first correspondence to final departure, professionalism and etiquette should go hand-in-hand on the job.

R·E·S·P·E·C·T

Respect should be shown from the ground up at work—from the attendant who parks your car to the high-powered CEO who signs your paycheck. But respect encompasses more than just remaining civil to that one coworker who is always trying to push her work off onto your plate, or has an annoying habit of sticking her finger in your ear in order to get your attention.

Arriving at work on time or, even better, five to ten minutes early each day is the easiest way to show respect in the workplace. It also guarantees you the freshest cup of coffee. So take *that*, late-coming coworkers.

> Disagreements are a given in the workplace, but you should never interrupt or speak over someone with whom you don't see eye to eye. Give him the chance to communicate his point and then express yours with the expectation of the same level of consideration. If he becomes discourteous and raises his voice, do not follow suit. **There's no such thing as Bring Your Inner Child to Work Day for a reason.**

> You may have a burning question for your boss, but it won't be answered any faster if you perch yourself on her desk while waiting for her to finish a phone call. If you see that a colleague you need to speak to is busy, wait until she is free before you make your approach. Nagging will get you nowhere except left off the invite list for after-work cocktails.

Dress for Success

Although many workplaces are adhering to a more "business casual" type of dress code, you should have your company's policy spelled out ahead of time. When interviewing for a new job, it's completely appropriate (and appreciated) to ask what the dress code is *before* arriving to your interview (even if it is a more casual environment, it's best to dress a bit more on the conservative side—especially for that first meeting).

> Even in the most laid-back of environments, there are definite no-nos for what is appropriate to wear to work. **Tank tops, shorts, way too worn-in jeans (especially those that are ripped or stained), graphic Ts, sneakers, flip-flops, and baseball caps are all best left for your weekend wear, assuming you don't work at Abercrombie & Fitch.**

> Unless you work in a body art shop, tattoos and piercings may be something your employers would rather not see. Ask your human resources rep whether you need to cover up or remove those piercings before the morning bell rings. Just make sure to do this at home—not at your desk.

Body Language

Your body language conveys as much about you in the workplace as the words you say or the clothing you wear.

> Whether meeting a potential boss for an interview or a longtime client for a business lunch, a firm handshake—one or two shakes while looking the directly person in the eye— communicates confidence and professionalism. Limp shakers

are looked at as weak or nervous, and those who hold on too tight or for too long can seem a bit over-confident or downright creepy. **Friendly waves are for beauty queens only**.

> Touching of any other nature—a squeeze here, a neck massage there—is strictly forbidden in a professional setting. So trash those "One Free Foot Rub" gift certificates you were planning to hand out as birthday gifts this year.

Noises Off

Noise—be it a constantly ringing cell phone or a colleague's one-octave-too-high voice—can be a productivity killer in the workplace. Particularly considering the open nature of many of today's office spaces, where the only thing that separates your from your neighbor is a carpeted partition, be conscious of the amount of noise that you create.

> As part of your morning ritual, just like those first few sips of coffee as you wait for your computer to warm up, turn your cell phone to vibrate (if the phone is used for work purposes and actually allowed in the office; otherwise, leave it in the car for use only during your lunch break). **And make sure to lose "Ding Dong the Witch Is Dead" as your boss's personalized ringtone**.

> We all know the sounds that alert us to an incoming e-mail. But like all those register "dings" at the grocery store, the combined sound of so many of them in close

quarters can be migraine-inducing. If you must have an audio indication that someone has sent you an e-mail, keep it as quiet as possible so as not to disturb those around you. Or inspire e-mail envy.

Be sure that any personal music being played if it's allowed in the first place is quiet enough that it's for your ears only. Not everyone in the office is likely to appreciate your fine taste in '80s hard rock. Unless expressly allowed, do not listen to your iPod or other listening instruments where headphones are required, either. It's too easy to get caught up in the music and not even notice when you're being addressed. Or that you've been singing along to "Sweet Caroline" for the past five minutes.

Business Meetings

Whether in person, over the phone, online, or via video chat, business meetings are a part of any job, regardless of the industry.

> If you have a meeting agenda, it's helpful—and efficient— for all those involved to receive this at least 24 hours ahead of time so that they can best prepare for the conversation ahead. That's also a perfect time to ask if the other attendees have anything they'd like to add to the day's agenda. And whether they prefer bagels or donuts.

> Sometimes meetings will run longer than expected, but try to schedule a time frame for how long any meeting will be and include that information in your confirmation (e.g., 11 to 12). This will help everyone keep focused during the meeting to discuss only those matters that are germane to the topic and scheduled agenda. **But be flexible if related issues that you hadn't anticipated are brought up in the course of conversation and need to be explored further (who won last night's football game is probably not one of those topics).**

Personal Matters

Dealing with a personal issue while at work can sometimes be unavoidable. But in today's technology-focused age, the line between a personal phone call or e-mail here and there and misuse of company time is a thin one. The best rule to follow? When you're at the office, you're on company time and all activities should be work-related.

> Even if part of your job requires updating your company's social networking pages on Facebook, Twitter, etc., this does not give you the right to check out what your friends are up to or view your sister's newly posted album of party pictures.

> It's common to become friendly outside of work with some of your colleagues, but always respect the office as a sacred place of "business only." Personal conversations between employees about their raucous weekend plans

together are distracting—and annoying—to others. Particularly when that conversation starts with, "Dude, I don't remember *anything* from last night. . ."

Non-work-related e-mail forwards are ubiquitous and a total waste of both the sender and recipient's time. Refrain from sending chain letters, jokes, and other forwards to your work colleagues, no matter how funny you may find them. Or how much money you're going to inherit if you can just forward this one message to 100 people in the next five minutes.

The Communal Kitchen

The main rule of the communal kitchen area is simple: clean up after yourself. This means wiping out the microwave when you've finished nuking your lunch, cleaning any dishes or silverware you've used as soon as you've finished with them, and mopping up any spills or other accidents that you have caused.

> Be conscious of the food you're bringing into the workplace. A tuna fish sandwich just like mom used to make may be what you're craving come noontime, but your scent-sensitive neighbors may not appreciate this nostalgic nod when it attacks their sense of smell—or their own lunches that are sharing space with it in the fridge.

Learn to Share

Unless you work from home, you'll more than likely have to deal with the challenges of shared equipment in the workplace, including fax machines, printers, copiers, and coffee makers.

> Don't be an equipment hog. Sometimes it's necessary to receive—and review—a 100-page contract via fax in a hurry. When possible, plan ahead for this sort of circumstance with an overnighted hard copy or by having the document scanned and e-mailed. **Save a tree and your colleagues' sanity.**

> Whether or not you're the one who printed that 100-page document, if the fax machine or printer runs out of ink/paper/whatever while you are using it, replenish its supply. **Don't be the office jerk who runs away and waits for the next person to do it.** This rule applies to anything in the office that can run out, including the coffee pot and water cooler. (There's no better way to show off all that time you've been putting in at the gym than hoisting a water cooler onto your shoulder. You too, ladies.)

> You've got three minutes to fax a dated document to the office in Tulsa but there's someone ahead of you in line? Never assume that you're the only person with an urgent document going out and push yourself to the front of the line. Whether it's one or ten people ahead of you, ask *everyone's* permission if it's okay for your message to take priority

before jumping ahead. Just pray it doesn't take four minutes to get everyone's blessing.

> If you happen to be sending a fax when an incoming document transmits for your colleague, save your coworker a little shoe leather and drop it off at his desk. But no peeking! You don't need to go overboard and become the office's Kris Kringle of received documents. But if it's there, and you have a moment, do your coworker a favor (and hope that it kicks off a new trend).

Pushing for That Promotion

When a senior-level position opens up and management has decided to promote from within, there will always be a winner and losers for the title. This is bound to lead to hurt feelings on the part of *someone*.

> In your campaign to win a better title, never forget the big picture—namely that you'll need to continue to work in a collaborative way with the candidates who don't get the job. Never play dirty. Resorting to low-down tricks and making sure office gossip about your competitors spreads to the higher-ups will only serve to make you look bad and dishonest. Imagine (but don't act as if) you have the promotion already, and treat your coworkers with the respect you would if you were now supervising. Who says it can't be a self-fulfilling prophecy?

> When the newly promoted candidate is announced, be humbled if you are crowned the winner but don't sulk if it's your office nemesis who got called up to the majors. If you're going to need to continue working with—and under—this person, a note or small token of congratulations—lunch on you, an after-work drink—can go a long way toward your future working relationship. If you are indeed victorious in your quest for a step up the corporate ladder, don't gloat. Always be gracious. This isn't a cutthroat reality show; the only reality here is that you'll need to work with these people for the foreseeable future—you'll need their respect. **Take a page out of the beauty pageant circuit in terms of how to win—or lose—with grace.**

Let's Talk about Sex

Nothing scares a company more than the words "sexual harassment lawsuit." Unlike more clear-cut offenses in the workplace—missing a deadline, falling asleep at your desk every afternoon at 3 P.M. on the dot—one can't always gauge what sort of discussion or action will offend a coworker. Which means that you should refrain from *any* sort of conversation/activity that could raise a red flag—whether you (or your boss) think it's all in good fun or not.

> The United States Equal Employment Opportunity Commission (EEOC) definition of sexual harassment includes explicit requests for sexual favors, threatening an employee's job if he or she doesn't perform the sexual requests being asked by the harasser, or speaking in a way that

could be deemed overtly sexual (even if not directed at the offended person). This last part is where you need to be careful, as it means an employee could claim sexual harassment as a result of hearing a coworker make an inappropriate joke to another. A perfect example of wrong place, wrong time.

> If you feel offended by something you've seen or heard in the workplace, the best first step is to address it directly with the harasser. Let this person know that you are offended by his conduct and would appreciate him refraining from such conversations/actions in the workplace in the future. The culprit may very well be just as embarrassed by the situation as you are—and have learned an important lesson in the meantime. If the behavior continues despite your previous conversation, address the matter with your boss (or, if it's your boss who is harassing you, go straight to your human resources representative).

Many offices have strict policies about dating in the workplace. Still, with the average American working 46 hours per week, it's hard to escape the fact that romantic feelings between coworkers can sometimes happen. If you find yourself in some sort of office romance, and you absolutely plan to see where it's going to go, speak with your boss or human resources representative about how you should address the issue. You don't have to hide your love away, but you do need to keep it in check. PDA has no place in the workplace.

CHAPTER 3

On the Road

❖❖❖❖❖❖❖❖❖❖❖❖❖❖❖❖✦❖❖❖❖❖❖❖❖❖❖❖❖❖❖❖❖

You may know the phrase "rules of the road," but do you know what those rules actually are? We're not talking about how many car lengths to remain behind the person in front of you, but the ways in which you can maintain civility at 55 mph and above.

Driving Basics

You may look good driving your car, but is what you're doing in that car good for the other folks on the road? **Well-mannered folks follow rules, meaning they abide by posted signs—including speed limits—and don't become bullies behind tinted glass windows.**

> ➤ We've all encountered those drivers who make us wonder how they passed a driving test in the first place. And it's easy to want to go all *Fast & Furious* on the sports car that cut you off. But two jackass drivers only increase the chance of an accident occurring and are a danger to everyone on the road. So take a deep breath when that Porsche zooms past you and rest easy in the assurance that *your* insurance premiums won't be going up next year.

> Most people are quick to forget proper hand signals once they've passed their driver's test. Luckily, unless you're driving the Flintstones' car, your automobile is equipped with some electronic signals that alert other drivers to what your plans are—slowing down, moving to the left or right, or that you're having some sort of car trouble. Use these handy-dandy gadgets liberally and whenever you're going to be making some sort of move that the drivers around you need to know about. But don't treat your signals as a be-all, end-all announcement to the world. Just because you signal doesn't mean that everyone is going to see it and move out of your way—or make way for you—immediately. The general rule is to signal five seconds or about 50 yards before you make your move. So plan ahead.

Once you've made your turn or exited, make sure that the signal has shut off. There's nothing more annoying than slowing down because you think the car ahead of you is trying to make its way to the right . . . for 10 miles down the highway. Like the car who cried turn, you could be in for a nasty bump when you actually *do* need to shift your position.

> In Driver's Utopia, everyone would let one car go before proceeding forward when merging. But there's always going to be that one hurried driver who just can't wait the extra three seconds to let another car go . . . just so he can get stuck behind the car in front of him again. Resist the urge to lay on your horn or give a middle-fingered wave to

these highway bullies. They all get what's coming to them sooner or later—including a massive insurance bill.

> Just as you'd (hopefully) thank someone who held a door open for you at the grocery store, always acknowledge courtesy on the road with a two-pronged wave: one when the driver signals you to move ahead and a second when you've completed your movement. **Two thank-yous are better than one.**

> Cell phone bans on the road are not a matter of the authorities wanting to limit your fun; it's about safety first. Even the shortest and most mindless of phone conversations takes some of your attention away from what you should be concentrating on—the road ahead—and as such increases the chances of an accident. If there's ever a phone call that you must take while on the road, pull over before answering. The lives of the other folks on the road depend on it.

> An even bigger danger nowadays is texting and driving. With a cell phone, you at least have the option of a handless headset and can keep your eyes on the road ahead of you. Texting requires two hands on the phone and a set of darting eyes. It's a recipe for a collision, which isn't a dish that anyone would request.

> Headlights are meant for one thing and one thing only: to help you see in dark or inclement weather. High beams can assist in really dark or inclement weather. **Nowhere in**

your driver's manual will you find "scaring the person in front of you to move to the slow lane" as an official use for your headlights.

> Similarly, your horn is meant to alert others to potential hazards on the road—an ajar door or diaper bag on the roof, for example. It's not meant to serve as your voice to other drivers, letting them know it's time to get out of the way to make room for you, no matter how cool your customized *Dukes of Hazzard* horn sounds.

Back-Seat Driving

When you've buckled into the back seat for a quick jaunt or a cross-country road trip, resist the urge to become the much-maligned—and very stereotypical—back-seat driver. You may have been a little more daring and taken that left into oncoming traffic, but shouting out something like "Go!" or "Now!" serves only to scare the bejesus out of the driver.

> The only time it's appropriate for a passenger to alert the driver to something is if there's a potential danger that you're not sure he sees, such as a car about to cross over into your lane. Even then, alert him in a calm and even voice; sudden outbursts aren't helpful to anyone. Let the driver do his job—you just sit back and enjoy the ride. You may know a great shortcut, but unless you're asked, keep that little secret to yourself.

> Don't offer to take over driving duties because there's a situation you don't think the driver can handle, such as parallel parking. **Be patient; you'll get where you're going and have a happier stay there if the driver isn't seething over your bossiness.**

A car is like a second home to its owner, so it's a place where he makes the rules. If this means seat belts on for the entire ride, do it. If this means no smoking, no problem. And if it means listening to the 17-minute rendition of "Disco Inferno" on repeat, so be it.

> Stay seated. Nothing's more distracting to a driver than kids (or adults) fighting in the back seat (just ask Mom and Dad). Stay put and save your arguments and attempts at backyard wrestling for your destination.

Road Trips

For longer trips, always make known your willingness to take over the driving duties if the driver wishes with a simple, "Just let me know if you'd like me to take over." But don't insist.

> If a friend offers up her car for a road trip, offer to pay for at least a tank of gas and tolls. She's the one accumulating mileage and wear and tear—and that tank of gas is likely to be much cheaper than a plane ticket. Yes, even with today's gas prices.

> If your road-tripping cohort does indeed agree to let you take the wheel, be sure to treat her car with the utmost respect. If someone is in such a hurry to get to his destination that he has to speed up to pass you and then cuts you off, don't you speed up to show him who's boss. You should want to create a distance between you and the driver; do everyone a favor and move out of his way so that you can continue to enjoy the open road. **Don't turn highway travel into the Indy 500.**

> Don't react to the driver who sneaks up on you and rides your bumper, or "pushes" you, on the road. Wait until it's safe for you to move into another lane and then do so. You're not giving in to the driver's intimidation; you're simply making the road a safer place for the rest of you. If the police don't catch up to him, karma certainly will.

> Make sure to indicate your intention to move out of this buffoon's way by turning your signal on. He should have enough respect for the rules of the road—or desire to not wreck his own car—to allow you a little bit of breathing room to safely change lanes.

Radio Signals

A car ride with the top down and the stereo blaring is a symbol of American freedom. It's also a distraction to others both on and off the road.

> Driving is as much about listening as it is about seeing. **You need to have the radio volume down low enough to hear any trouble that might be brewing in the form of horns blaring, brakes screeching, or an impromptu circus on the road.** Your car radio should never be loud enough for the cars around you—or pedestrians on the sidewalk—to make out the song.

> If you've got passengers in the car, don't be a radio hog—even if it is your car and you're the one driving. Settle on a station that everyone can enjoy, or play the "your turn, my turn" game where everyone gets a chance to control the radio for a set period of time.

> Unless Lady Gaga is riding shotgun, resist the urge to turn a car ride into mobile karaoke. Your mom may think you've got a wonderful voice, but your friends might take a more critical view of your pipes.

Blow Your Horn

Remember those "Honk If You're [Fill in the Blank]" bumper stickers that were popular decades ago? Even the drivers who plastered those on their bumpers meant it as a tongue-in-cheek kind of thing. There's no more annoying sound on the road than a steady stream of car horns blasting. The horn's sole purpose is to keep the roads safe around you. If you see what could be an impending disaster about to happen, honk your horn to alert the drivers around you.

> Even the most expensive cars have blind spots. If you notice a car starting to make its way into your lane—into the very same space you're occupying—a quick toot will let him know that "this lane is occupied, buddy" without the snarky attitude.

> Short, to-the-point beeps are the appropriate way to send out a warning; holding your hand down on the horn for 30 seconds isn't going to get your point across any clearer. It's only going to annoy all those around you.

Pull Over

No one hits the road with the intention of being pulled over by a police officer. But many people have a weird tendency to turn indignant when this happens.

> Don't forget the role of the police officer in society: to avoid civil disobedience. If you truly feel that you were pulled over in error, the time to express that is in court. Don't waste more time pulled over on the side of the road by arguing your point. If you feel that you were wrongfully ticketed, take it to court; the info on how to do that is readily available on the ticket itself. In the meantime, be served with a smile.

> Before you launch into a barrage of excuses, give the officer the floor. You'll never know why he pulled you over unless you let him talk first. **Who wants to offer up that "Yes, officer, I** did **have a beer at lunch . . ." when he**

merely wanted to let you know that your gas tank was open.

> If you are a passenger in the car, do not assume the role of King of the Road and complain, argue, or try to bully the officer. You're not the one receiving—or paying—the ticket, so you have no right to play the role of debate team captain.

Park It

The purpose of a parking lot—a place where cars remain stationary—may make it seem like an odd place for fender benders, but they're one of the places where drivers seems to forget the rules of the road. With everyone jockeying for position for a spot closest to the entrance, a crowded parking lot is a recipe for driver altercations galore.

> Unless you're disabled—in which case you should apply for a handicapped plate—the easiest way to emerge from a parking lot scar-free is to park in the emptiest portion and simply walk further to your destination. A little walking never hurt anyone. And you'll probably save time by going straight to the faraway spot as opposed to waiting for a closer spot to open up anyway. If you see an open spot and also see someone signaling for it, resist the temptation to hit that turbo button and zoom on in. **Parking is a first-come, first-served sport. Hate the game, not the players.**

> If you notice someone waiting for your spot, don't take your sweet old time leaving. Yes, make sure your packages are secure and that you and your passengers are safely buckled in. But now is not the time to call your long-lost second cousin and check out the latest NASDAQ numbers on your phone. Parking spots are temporary homes for your car while you attend to business; when you're done, make your way out of the lot and let someone else move in.

It's not okay to park your Humvee in three compact spots. Park your car in only those spots where the car actually fits between the lines *and* leaves room for you and your neighboring cars to open your doors to emerge. The insurance costs of denting a car aren't worth the extra two minutes it would take for you to keep driving and find an appropriate spot. In the case of that Humvee, the appropriate spot would be "tank-sized."

> It may seem obvious, but it's certainly worth stating for the record: if you are not handicapped, you cannot park in a handicapped spot. Remember, disabilities aren't always visible to the naked eye. Never take it upon yourself to question someone's legal right to utilize a handicapped or otherwise designated spot. Leave that up to the authorities to sort out—and fine appropriately.

> Even if your vehicle has a handicapped plate because a member of your family is disabled, if that person is not with

you, the plate doesn't make it okay to take a reserved spot. Some lots even include elderly and expectant mother spots near the door. Don't take liberties with your beer belly and hope that no one will ask.

> Parking lots require proper behavior from pedestrians, too. Don't saunter down the middle of the lot, making it impossible for cars to pass you on either side. Stick to one side of the lot so that cars can easily pass you, but don't walk so close to the parked cars that you don't see someone backing out (or they don't see you). All the double coupons in the world aren't going to make *that* a worthwhile trip to the store.

> When utilizing a shopping cart, always return the cart to the safety of the cart catchers in the middle of the lot. **An empty parking space is not an appropriate place to park your cart.** Don't try arguing the equal rights of a shopping cart as a moving vehicle, either.

Taxicab Confessions

In big cities like New York, taxis are a way of life—and a source of much frustration. Dangerous driving habits and congested roadways are just two of the reasons they make life more difficult, but they're sometimes the only way to get around.

> The old two-fingers-in-the-mouth whistle may be the only talent you need to perfect to hail a cab in the movies, but which city you're standing in is what really dictates how you'll hail a cab. In some places, getting a cab is as easy as making a quick phone call and telling them your destination or finding a designated taxi queue. In other cities, again, like New York, you simply need to walk to the curb with your hand outstretched and up high and wait for the first cab to pull up in front of you (the one with only its middle light on, which indicates that it's unoccupied and open for business).

> Hailing a cab can sometimes be an exercise in patience (especially when the weather is anything but sunny and warm). No matter how late you're running, it's never okay to steal a cab from another person. Even if you *were* waiting before her, if the driver pulls up to another passenger, that cab belongs to her. If you'd like to take a chance on splitting the cab, simply ask to see if you're headed in the same direction and whether she'd mind sharing a cab. It's a money-saving option for both of you—and an eco-friendly one, as well. If she balks at the request, fugghetaboutit.

> As a cab passenger, you have rights—and you should know them. Often they're posted right there in front of your face. **If your driver does anything to violate these rules—is driving erratically, plays his music at ear-shattering decibels, refuses to turn the heat on even though your fingers have turned into icicles—you**

have the right to ask him to correct his behavior. If he refuses, your tip should reflect that shoddy service, and a call to the local taxi commission (this number, too, should be posted with your rights) is definitely in order. Don't forget to write down all of the driver's information—his name, license number, and medallion number—before exiting the vehicle.

Commuter Courtesies

For all the luxuries driving yourself to work each day offers, commuting offers its own little luxuries: less pollution, no car payments, and the ability to read a book or watch a movie as you make your way to the office.

> Whether commuting by train or bus, don't cut in line. (Are you sensing a theme here?) For safety and sanity, line up in an orderly fashion. When the door(s) open, wait until everyone has exited the vehicle before boarding. And even then, don't make a mad dash for the nearest seat, pushing an old lady out of the way so that you can get to the one remaining seat before she does. Seating is on a first-come, first-served basis. If you're lucky enough to find one, be willing to give it up for an elderly or disabled person or pregnant woman. And remember: seats are for your behind, not your belongings. **If your bowling bag didn't pay to ride, it doesn't have the right to occupy a seat.**

> If you're feeling at all under the weather, do *everyone* a favor and stay home. If you must travel—to your doctor's office, hopefully—make sure you're well supplied with tissues, cough drops, and whatever else you may need to not infect your fellow passengers.

If your seating options include squeezing in between two people or seizing the wide-open luxury of the designated handicapped seating, squish. It will save you from possibly having to get up (and lose your seat altogether) later. If someone asks you to move over so that she can sit down (and there is space to do just that), make the room sans eye rolls.

> Silence is golden: if you're listening to music or watching a movie, wear headphones. If you're embroiled in a game of Angry Birds, turn the sound off. Similarly, if you *must* make or receive a phone call during your commute, do so as quietly as possible. No one needs your business to be broadcast, particularly as they're trying to stay out of the "work zone" until arriving at their own places of employment.

CHAPTER 4

On Vacation

You can take a vacation from a lot of things—your job, your marriage, your best friend, your family. But what you can't (or shouldn't) leave behind are your good manners.

Planes, Trains, and Etiquette

The general behavioral rules for airline and railway travel are pretty similar—in both cases, you're trapped in a tight seat for several hours. Don't forget to pack your patience.

> A strange thing happens when it comes to air travel: people are tripping over themselves and the other passengers to board, and then can't disembark quickly enough. As might be expected from a high-tech industry like aeronautics, there *is* a system to how you are boarded—and it's not just so you can watch those fancy-pants first-class passengers parade on by. Stay seated in the waiting area until your row has been called for boarding. Don't crowd the pathway to the gate in anticipation of that magic moment when you're invited to board. It only creates a human traffic jam that results in you waiting longer to board—and to depart for your destination (which hopefully is a tropical one).

> When you arrive at your own row, stow your bags into the appropriate place—overhead or under the seat—quickly and sit down so that the people in line behind you can do the same thing. Offer to help any elderly or disabled individuals or any families with children. You'll be doing everyone on the plane a favor by helping get bags stowed and passengers into their seats more quickly. If storing baggage under the seat, make sure you're doing so under only the seat directly in front of you—don't take liberties and think the entire row is yours (unless you've got your own private plane).

> If you know your "carry on" bag is not going to fit into even the largest of overhead bins, check it before boarding. No one wants to pay an extra $30 to check in a piece of oversized luggage, but you're never going to sneak it past the flight attendants or other travelers. **So suck it up and check it (and make sure to do a better edit of your wardrobe next time).**

> You never know what might set off an allergy—or annoyance—in the people around you. When you know you'll be flying, refrain from spritzing yourself wildly with your favorite musk. Similarly, avoid packing a lunch that can stink up the plane in a matter of minutes (we're looking at you, tuna salad).

> Before you push that seat into a recline position, take a quick peek at who—if anyone—is behind you and how your preferred angle of recline might affect him. If you

notice his kneecaps touching his chin, lessen the recline a bit. With such limited room in the first place, there's really no difference between an upright position and a "reclined" one anyway.

> Keep your feet planted firmly on the ground. Airplanes and movie theaters run a tight race for most infuriating place to have someone constantly kicking the seat behind you.

If you're traveling with a companion, don't forget that this isn't a charter flight. Just because you've got a lot of catching up to do doesn't mean the rest of the plane wants to hear your recollections of all your high school hijinks. Keep your voices down so that your conversation remains private.

> Hey, did you hear? Smoking was banned during airline travel two decades ago. Sure, it may look cool (to smokers, that is) when you watch those old movies. But don't try it nowadays or you're liable to end up in handcuffs.

> Just because you forgot your book doesn't mean you can use the stranger sitting next to you as your in-flight entertainment. There are generally two types of flyers: the talkative types and the loners. If it's clear from the initial salutation that you're on opposing teams, leave the person alone. If you become the target for a talkative stranger, don't be afraid to put them off—politely, of course. Some people talk incessantly out of nervousness on a flight. This

is one situation where it's helpful to have an iPod or book handy; both provide a legitimate excuse to cut your conversation short. Just don't blow your cover by holding your reading materials upside down.

> If you do have an iPod or other personal electronic device that makes noise, *always* wear headphones. If you forgot them, you're out of luck, because it's never permissible to make the volume public—not even at the lowest level. If you do wear headphones, still keep the noise to a minimum. That random bass sound that emanates from someone's headphones is more annoying than hearing the actual music.

> If you're lucky enough to have a personal video device—or are on a plane with individual television sets—be mindful of your flying companions. **The five-year-old sitting next to you may not appreciate your taste in slasher movies—and may not sleep for a week afterward.**

> If someone asks you to switch seats to be nearer to his or her travel companion, do yourself a favor and say yes. Otherwise you're going to literally be in the middle of their conversation the entire trip. Better yet, don't wait to be asked—offer up the courtesy. Even if your motivations are selfish, you'll impress fellow travelers with your seemingly random act of kindness.

> Given its unexpected turbulence, an airplane is really not an ideal place to eat or drink. It's all too easy—and common—for food to go flying everywhere, including into your neighbor's lap. Whether you think it's the pilot's fault or that pesky storm cloud you're making your way through, if *your* food or beverage spills on to your neighbor's lap, it's *your* fault. Do what you can to help mitigate the damage and offer to pay for any dry cleaning bills. Also: never forget that alcohol affects people more intensely at high altitudes. A cocktail to calm the nerves is one thing; having to be helped off the plane is not acceptable.

> Don't risk being thrown off the plane (or spending your vacation in the clink) by giving lip to the flight attendants. Even if they *are* all out of peanuts.

Bus Trip

Buses offer an economical way to see the world at a fraction of the cost—and with the luxury of your very own personal driver. But they also feature pretty tight quarters, where personal space is at a premium.

> If you're planning on sleeping most of the journey, grab a seat at the front of the bus. If you plan to chat with your cohorts or take more of an active role on the trip—getting a wave started or something—the back of the bus is where you want to be. It's an unwritten rule of the road.

> In inclement weather particularly, give your shoes a good cleaning with the help of the sidewalk to remove any snow, salt, or water before boarding. And don't place your soaking-wet coat or umbrella on the seat next to you, rendering it virtually un-sittable for a fellow passenger (even if that *was* your intention).

> If you enter an empty row of seats, make your way to the window so that it's clear the seat next to you is open and easy for a fellow passenger to squeeze right in. Don't put your bag or other belongings on the seat next to you in an attempt to fool people into believing that you're traveling with a companion. The truth will come out soon enough—as soon as you depart the station.

> Most bus lines prohibit the use of cell phones. Don't be the guy who thinks the rules don't apply to him. Especially when you're the only one talking, you're rendering the entire bus hostage to your phone conversation. And you never want to be the passenger singled out by the driver over the loudspeaker.

Cruising

Long-time cruisers like to get all fancy and talk about "embarkation." This is just a fancy word for "when you get on the ship." Regardless of how early you purchased your tickets or how much your cabin is costing you, be prepared to wait while boarding a ship. Thousands of people are setting sail with you and each one of them needs to go through the same individual check-in process, so be patient and consider it part of the journey.

When it comes to food, today's cruise ships are known for having plenty of it all day and night. Don't get so wrapped up in the cuisine that you lose your manners pushing into line to snag that last pecan sandy or screaming at the man ahead of you who can't make up his mind between the chicken or the beef. Some decisions require some serious soul-searching.

> There's more to setting sail on the high seas than all-you-can-eat buffets. World-class entertainment in various forms is just a few steps away at every turn. If this vacation is a family trip, be aware of the sort of entertainment you're getting yourself into. Casinos that feature gambling and lounges with lewd comedy acts are no place for Little Billy to spend his evenings.

> Attention smokers: just because there's no roof above your head when you're on deck doesn't mean you can light up freely. Be sure to locate the ship's designated smoking areas and relegate your nicotine habit to those sections only. Also note: the ocean is not the world's largest garbage receptacle; do not take it upon yourself to dispose of your cigarettes or that unwanted last plate of food from the buffet overboard. There are trash cans aplenty on large ships.

Hotels and Motels

The start of any vacation begin with lines—first it's the airport, then it's the hotel. Never forget the subtle art of being patient; lots of other happy folks are in the same boat as you—on vacation—so set the tone with a positive check-in. And keep smiling no matter how long it takes to finally get that key.

> You expect your room to be clean and well-stocked when you arrive at a hotel, right? Well, don't put an extra burden on the housekeeping staff by not allowing them enough time to clean up after your departure. Check-in and check-out times are standard and should be followed. If you attempt to arrive two hours prior to the posted check-in time and are informed your room is not ready, don't make a stink about it. Simply check your bags with the concierge and start your vacation exploration a little early—leave the paperwork for later. If you can't get yourself up and out the door by the posted check-out time, float this by the front desk first. Some hotels do charge extra for a late check-out. In which case, pay the fee with a smile—you're the one who's making their work harder.

> Sure, you're on vacation. You want to kick back, relax, and get away from the daily grind of your everyday life. That doesn't include taking a vacation from your manners. Treat your hotel room as if you were staying in a friend's apartment, keeping in mind that there are other guests (also trying to enjoy their stay) on every side of you. **Keep the noise level to a minimum—and resist the urge to treat the**

bed like a trampoline out of sheer giddiness that you've got an entire week off.

> If you're traveling with children, keep close tabs on them for everyone's sake. The sound of kids running wildly up and down a hotel hallway—or hopping in the elevator and pressing all the buttons—may be a cute story for you to tell when you get home, but it ruins the experience for the hotel's other guests. Just as you would come ready with distractions in the form of board games, etc. on a long road trip, pack supplies to keep your kids occupied.

If you booked a nonsmoking room or end up *in* a nonsmoking room don't light up. You may not be able to smell it, but the next guest will surely not appreciate that the Marlboro Man slept here.

> If you're being bothered by disorderly hotel guests—out-of-control kids, a blaring television set, a fighting couple—register a complaint with the front desk and a hotel staffer will take care of it. Don't attempt to address the problem on your own, either face-to-face or with a few swift knocks on the wall.

The B&B Way

Somewhere between a hotel stay and a weekend at a friend's house is bed-and-breakfast living. Part of a B&B's charm is its intimacy. You're staying in someone's home, after all, not a high-tech hotel with all the latest gadgetry. Creaking floorboards, hissing pipes, and noises from the guests around you are just a few of the sounds you can expect to hear.

> The best way to think about a B&B stay is to act as if you're the guest of a guest at a family friend's house. Expect warm hospitality, comfortable sleeping quarters, home-cooked meals, and some local experts on the area from your hosts. The B&B is your hosts' actual home. Treat your surroundings accordingly. Afford them the same respect you would anyone you were trying to impress with the hope of being invited back.

> Don't tote Fido along and think that all will be okay. A B&B could have several reasons for not being pet-friendly—including an allergic owner—so don't try and "sneak" the little guy in and hope that no one will notice. Always make sure your accommodations are pet-friendly *before* you arrive.

> If you're running late for your check-in time, call the owners to let them know. They have lives outside of work, too. You want to make sure that someone is there to greet you—or at the very least, hand you a key.

Great Outdoors

For those souls courageous enough to brave the wilderness for a camping trip, don't think there aren't certain rules that apply to you, too. At the end of the day, a camping trip is a B&B stay in Mother Nature's home. You need to respect your surroundings even more than you would the local Holiday Inn; the outdoors don't offer maid service.

> The main rule of camping is "If you carry it in, carry it out." Keeping your campsite clean is a must. Don't leave food or other items that might attract wild animals, and make sure you're not doing anything that might damage your surroundings. Do this out of respect for your surroundings—and your life if the neighborhood bears come calling.

> It's not just nature you need to respect; it's your fellow campers, too. Noise carries in the wild almost more than anywhere. So keep your voices—and any musical accompaniment—for your ears only. **Don't walk through other campsites, walk around them (even if your neighbor's site does provide a much-needed shortcut to the restrooms).**

Getting Hostel

Of all the accommodations you could choose for your adventure, a hostel requires good manners more than any (*and* a working set of earplugs).

> You've chosen a hostel for one reason or another—probably price. And just because the environment is casual, that doesn't mean you own the place. Show the utmost respect for your fellow travelers; keep the noise down when you're coming and going—especially those early-morning or late-night jaunts. If you want to wax philosophical at 2 A.M., do it outside, where you won't disturb your dorm mates. And keep the lights off—literally—with those early-morning and late-night comings and goings. **You don't want to be the one who wakes up an entire roomful of weary, hung-over travelers.**

> Many hostels are notoriously understocked when it comes to kitchenware—mainly because of the time and energy it takes to clean up after so many people. Do yourself and everybody else you're cozying up to a favor and clean up after yourself. It only takes a few extra seconds, and karma is bound to reward you with a clean fork when you really need it.

> If your plans change at the last minute—you meet a good-looking millionaire who invites you to stay at his palace—call the hostel and let them know you won't be coming. Free up one more bed for your impoverished, jet-setting brethren.

> Let's not beat around the bush on this one: as romantic as the idea of travel in a strange land may be, there's nothing sexy about getting busy with a stranger (or your traveling companion) in a dorm room full of other folks. **Save**

the stuff you should be doing behind closed doors for when you're the only two behind those closed doors.

Couch Surfing

A relatively new trend, couch surfing is the practice of crashing on the couch of not a friend, but a stranger, with the plan that you'll offer up your own living room at some point in return.

> Never arrive empty-handed. A small token of your appreciation—a bottle of wine, a nice candle, or a trinket from your hometown—is a great way to set the tone for a positive experience. Your host is doing this because he feels he has something to gain, too—mostly, meeting new and interesting folks—so be sure to set aside some time every day to chat with him. Get to know who he is. Ask him for recommendations on things to see/do/eat. Better yet: invite him along and pick up coffee.

> As you won't know how well you're going to get along with your host until you've actually arrived, a three-day stay is really the most you'll want to commit to from the get-go. Unless the host makes the offer, do not ask to extend your stay mid-visit. If things are going along swimmingly once you arrive and you're asked to board longer, you can accept the invitation without hesitation or reservation.

> Make yourself invisible. Never use something that doesn't belong to you without asking first. Your host clearly doesn't mind sharing—he's giving a perfect stranger his couch, after all—so it shouldn't be a problem. But it's polite to ask first anyway. Clean up after yourself each morning and leave no evidence that there's a guest in the house. If you're sleeping on a pull-out sofa, push the bed in and neaten the area each morning. Let the house be a house during the day and your crash pad in the evening.

Abroad

The best trips are those where your actions and appearance don't scream "tourist." Just as you probably researched the best deal on your airfare and hotel before planning your trip, you should also research the local customs and practices so that you can prepare to immerse yourself in a new culture before you leave.

Proper attire is one of the easiest ways to blend into your surroundings. We're not talking about a Halloween costume here, but if you're traveling in a conservative area, you'll want to leave your crop tops and skinny jeans at home. What passes for sexy at your local dive bar can be highly offensive on non-American soil.

> While it may seem awkward to do so, always address people formally—Mr. and Mrs. Phelps, not Gary and Linda—until you are given permission to be on a first-name

basis. If you're spending time in a country where you don't speak the language fluently, take the time to learn a few common phrases—"Hello," "Goodbye," "Please," "Thank you," and "Where is the bathroom?" can all come in handy.

> Just as at home, gratuities are a way of life in many service industries abroad. Always be prepared to tip for good service—and make sure you understand when to tip and how much so you don't insult your waiter (or give him enough for early retirement).

> It's also wise to understand a culture's views toward women so you're not surprised and insulted if treated in a way that you deem less than respectful as an American. Many foreign countries are still very much male-dominated (no matter what the ladies tell you).

CHAPTER 5

Eating Out

If you've ever had the experience of meeting someone whom you quickly grow to like . . . only to have that goodwill disappear when you've shared a meal in public with that person, you know the importance of restaurant etiquette. Whether you're with a business client, first date, future in-laws, or old friends, the dinner table is set with etiquette pitfalls that are easy to fall into and hard to escape. The good news is that poor dining etiquette is probably one of the easiest manners-related issues to fix.

Some Reservations

Unless you're dining out at your favorite little neighborhood spot, making reservations ahead of time is always a good idea. It lessens the possibility of any waiting time once you arrive at the restaurant and gives you the chance to make any special requests, such as outdoor seating, a private banquette in the back, or ten table lengths from any diners with kids.

> Reservations help the restaurant staff better plan for the evening's diners; they know whether it will be a slow

or busy night and can staff accordingly. If you need to cancel your reservations, make sure to call the restaurant and let them know—whether it's a week ahead of time or ten minutes after your scheduled seating. **They'll get the picture once you're a no-show, but why leave other patrons waiting for a table when they could be chowing down on a bread basket that was meant for you?**

> If you have to make any changes to the details of your reservations—you've gained or lost a guest or now need a table in the smoking section—call the restaurant as soon as possible so they can accommodate this change before you arrive. An extra person may not seem like a big deal to you, but it can be if there's no extra chair to speak of in the restaurant. (Even the shortest member of your party can't squeeze into a high chair.)

> If the restaurant balks at your changed request, don't become indignant. Dining out is a business based on accommodation and you can be sure that if it were possible, they would do it. *You're* the one who is changing your request at the last minute. How would you like it if the chef decided to switch the menu from carnivore to vegetarian just a few minutes before you arrived?

Drink Menu

A bottle of wine can be a festive way to celebrate a special occasion—even if that occasion is just a chance to catch up with a friend. It can also be a way to save a few dollars, believe it or not. If you imagine that you and your guest will each have two glasses of wine, do the math on a bottle of wine versus four glasses and see who comes out on top. A bottle of wine is the equivalent of about four and a half to five glasses, depending on who's pouring (and drinking).

> If the restaurant employs a sommelier, don't be afraid to ask for her recommendation, even if you do fancy yourself a grape connoisseur. Wine is the sommelier's life (not to mention her job). If you tell her which flavors or types of wine you like (say, fruity with a hint of spice), she can often make an amazing selection and introduce you to a varietal that you may not have tried otherwise.

> There's no reason to be shy about your price point when choosing a bottle of wine. Some wine drinkers think they're being tactful by always ordering the *second* least expensive wine on the list. But the flavors of the cheapest wine might be better suited to your palate. **If a bouquet is on a menu's wine list, they're recommending it, so don't be afraid to save a few dollars for fear of looking like a cheapskate.** Leave that to the people who split an entrée and only drink tap water.

> The first taste of wine will go to whomever chose the bottle. If you're tasting and the beverage is to your liking, nod your approval to the sommelier, who will then pour it for the rest of the table. If the wine is not to your liking, say

so. There's no use in choking down an entire bottle of wine you don't like—they let you taste it for a reason, sort of like a stomped-grape test drive.

If a member of your party refrains from imbibing, don't question her decision or have any further conversation about it. And don't automatically assume she's pregnant. There are a variety of reasons for even the biggest partier to abstain from drinking on occasion, such as that she's still nursing this morning's hangover.

Dressed to Impress

Appropriate attire speaks worlds about your character. While jacket-and-tie required establishments are certainly not the norm, they do still exist. Always check the dress code of a restaurant you'll be eating at (go to its website or make a quick phone call) and abide by that request. **You may feel that you're entitled to wear your pajama bottoms wherever you want because you're picking up the check, but there are others to consider in your quest to end up on *People*'s worst-dressed list—namely your dining companions.**

> Hats are never to be worn indoors—unless that indoor place happens to be a religious ceremony that calls for some sort of symbolic headwear (NBA Championship games included).

Ordering Basics

It's easy to get distracted talking when you first arrive at a restaurant. Don't forget that there's a menu to be reviewed and, on the part of the restaurant, a schedule to keep in terms of how long you'll be occupying the table. Don't take up twenty minutes with chitchat and then place your drink order. There will be plenty of time to talk once the business of eating has been attended to—and even after you've left the restaurant, if you wish.

> If even just one member of your party is not sure about what to order, ask the waiter to give you a couple of minutes. No one wants to feel pressured to make a quick dining decision, especially when making up your mind between the barbecue nut loaf or the tofu club.

> Never demand things from the wait staff with phrases like "Give me the grilled branzino." Be as polite as you would when someone is offering to make you a meal, for example, "May I please start out with a bowl of clam chowder? Then I'd like the steak mafia. Thank you."

Quiet, Please

Besides the great grub, one of the pleasures of a night out at a restaurant is the chance to catch up with someone while being catered to by a full staff.

> Few things can make this harder to do than a restaurant where the noise level is more akin to toga night at a frat

house. Sometimes this is a case of extra-loud patrons; other times it is a result of poor sound design within the space (such as high ceilings). If you're in a group of people, keeping the noise level in check is a more difficult task, but it is even more imperative to keep the folks around you happy. **Ten people all trying to deliver the punch line to an inside joke at the same time can wreak havoc on the eardrums of the restaurant's other patrons.** Do your part to keep the noise level in check by keeping your conversation just loud enough for only the people you're speaking with to hear.

> Many restaurants have rules against cell phone usage. Even if they're not posted, think of a restaurant as sacred ground—a place that technology should not enter. If you must make or accept a phone call, go to the lobby or outside to do this. And, for Pete's sake, set the phone to vibrate before you enter these hallowed eating grounds!

Unless you've got Brangelina sitting next to you, don't eavesdrop on others' conversations, no matter how juicy they may seem. (Okay, it would be rude to do it to Brad and Angie, too, but who could help themselves?)

Mind Your Manners

If you decide to disobey every other golden rule of dining—don't chew with your mouth open, don't talk with food in your mouth, don't eat with your hands—you can at least score brownie points for using a napkin correctly.

> The time to shift your napkin from plate to lap is once you've finished ordering and the waiter has removed your menus. Your napkin isn't just for the grand finale—it's wise to wipe your mouth throughout the meal (and at least between courses). **And remember: the napkin always goes in your lap—not around your neck (even if you order the lobster).**

> You don't need an etiquette class to figure out which utensils to use; there's a built-in cheat sheet in their placement: start with the one that is farthest from your plate and work your way to the inside (stopping short of your plate, obviously).

> Your bread plate and water glass don't have it so easy. Don't be the buffoon who drinks from the wrong water glass (especially after its rightful owner has already taken a swig). Bread to the left, water to the right.

> You might be famished, but never begin eating until everyone at the table has been served. And no matter how hungry you are, don't take it upon yourself to turn your companions' food into your own personal tasting menu, stabbing whatever looks good around the table. If it's a group of close friends, you can ask to try their dishes—although it's always more polite to wait until it is offered up. **If it's a business meal or new acquaintances, don't ask for a sample, no matter how yummy it all looks.**

> If you've got the feeling that there's something stuck in your tooth, don't shove a fork in there and go fishing. Excuse yourself (opening your mouth as little as possible) and make your way to the restroom, where you can try flushing it out with a mouthful of water. Just try not to dribble water on your tie.

Wait Staff Etiquette

The wait staff is there to serve you, true, but they've got other folks to attend to as well. When your waiter comes over to offer a hello, be sure to make eye contact and make note of his name. There's nothing more disrespectful to a waiter than having a patron ask—at the end of a ninety-minute nosh session—"Excuse me, are *you* my waiter?"

> Mind your Ps and Qs when the waiter approaches. If you and your companions are involved in a heavy-duty discussion, put it on hold when he approaches and only resume it once he's out of earshot. Your waiter doesn't need to hear about your sister's marital woes.

Check, Please

Who pays for a meal can be figured out pretty easily from how the plan came about. Did you invite someone for sushi? Did your boss invite you for lunch to celebrate your new promotion? The person who puts the invite out there should expect to pay for the meal. In more casual situations— best friends, your roommate—there can be an unsaid rule of going Dutch or maybe taking turns paying.

If you want to make it clear that you are the one paying for dinner, say that in your invite "I'd like to take you out to dinner for your birthday." That way, there's no football tackle for the bill at the end of the night.

> Arguing with a dining companion over who is going to pay the check makes everyone uncomfortable—including the server—and can quickly ruin the generosity with which the dining date was made in the first place. It is perfectly acceptable—required, really—that the person who did the inviting pays the check.

> There are some people who get highly competitive about the bill, either because they have trouble letting someone else pay for their meal or because they want to look like a big shot. A good way to avoid this from the get-go is to let the waiter know (privately) that you are going to be paying and ask him to please hand the bill to you, or to give him your credit card right then and there. That way, when the check arrives, it has already been paid—no argument necessary.

> If you have invited someone out for a meal, make sure you have enough money to cover the check. It would be terribly embarrassing to have to ask him to pay for his own birthday meal. If someone invites you out and tells you to pick the place, don't take this as a license to dine at Chez Expensivo on someone else's dime. Either defer to the inviter—"Please, *you* pick the place—I'd love to try one of your favorite restaurants!"—or be sure to choose a restaurant (and order an item) that is reasonably priced. It doesn't need to have a drive-through window, but a place where a burger is on the menu is always a safe bet.

> If you're trying to grab a quick meal before a movie or a show, ask your waiter for the check once the food arrives, or even when you're placing the order, so that it comes out with the food. That way, when it's ten minutes to showtime, there's no need to chase down your waiter. The restaurant staff is not going to let you leave without paying (that is, not without getting the cops involved).

> If you don't see your waiter or aren't able to get his attention with your well-practiced insistent smile (you know, when you give him *that* look), ask another waiter if he can send your server over when he has a minute. Don't be impatient or rude. And don't interrupt your server while he's waiting on another table. **Your table is not more important than any other. It's a different story if you're well known as a 40-percent tipper.**

> Of course, even in the finest restaurants, service doesn't always go smoothly. Just because your waiter seems to be in a bad mood doesn't mean you need to jump on the bandwagon. At the end of the day, arguing with your waiter will do nothing to improve your service, or your impression of a particular restaurant. If you're unhappy with your experience—the food took too long, your waiter seemed to have forgotten about you, a mouse ran over your foot—these are matters that fall under the manager's jurisdiction. That is the person with whom you should speak. The manager is also the one with the power to comp or not to comp (which can help make up for a less-than-stellar meal). The only thing worse than eating a bad meal is having to pay for that meal.

> Don't stiff the waiter, even if his service was crummy. Remember what the waiter's actual job is—to take your order, deliver it to the kitchen, bring it to your table, and hand you the check. He's not cooking the food so he has no control over how quickly it comes out or how well it is seasoned. And that seemingly bad attitude? It could be because he has no control over those things! **A 10–15 percent tip conveys your dissatisfaction—a zero percent tip conveys your classlessness.**

> When dining with a group, it is generally accepted that the bill will be split equally. The one exception is when you're celebrating a special occasion—say, a couple's engagement—in which case the rest of the party should split the tab for the guests of honor. One caveat here: if

you've been feasting on Johnnie Walker Blue while the rest of the table is splitting draft pitchers, it's a classy move (on par with that scotch you're drinking) to offer to up your share accordingly.

> On the other end of the splitting the bill spectrum, there's often the person who feels shortchanged: "But I only had a salad and didn't drink anything." If anyone seems resistant to split the bill equally, don't make a big deal about it. Total up the exact items this person consumed, with a little extra for tip, and have her pay that amount. It's not worth ending the night on a bad note for the few extra dollars it will cost the rest of the table. (Although you may want to lose her before heading over to the venue you'll be hitting up next.)

Entertaining

Whether you're throwing it or simply attending, who doesn't like a good party? And whether you're the host or the guest, your goal should be the same: to have a little fun. This might be easier said than done when you're in charge, but it's easy to plan well enough ahead of time that you can sit down and actually enjoy the party. After all, if you can't be a guest at your own shindig, what's the point of throwing one?

Invite Only

An official invitation to a party can come in many forms—in person, over the phone, via e-mail, or by way of the United States Postal Service. While it's always great to find a printed invitation nestled among the junk mail in your mailbox, it's not always completely necessary.

> Whether or not to send a written invitation—and how formal that invitation should be—is really up to the host. But it can be dictated by the event. A great rule to follow is that if there is a specific theme (ugly sweater party), special instructions (it's a surprise!), or gift registry information (a

bridal or baby shower), a written invitation can serve as a tangible FAQ—and a convenient reminder of the event that invited guests can stick on the fridge. That way, even the most forgetful of friends don't have an excuse for missing it.

> However you decide to invite people, be sure to let them know the date, start time, location, directions, dress code (if there is one), special instructions, RSVP date, and contact info. Even if you decide to keep the party going a little bit longer the night of the event, it's never a bad idea to include a start and end time to any sort of at-home affair. This gives guests a better idea of how to plan for the event (such as letting a babysitter know how long they'll be out) and to not feel like a total pooper if the party is still raging and they need to head home to bed.

> When it comes to creating an invite list, there are two things to consider: the celebration at hand and who is likely to be offended if he doesn't make the cut. If it's a very specific celebration—a 60th surprise party for your mom, for example—you'll have a pretty easy guest list of friends and family members. **If it's something a little more open-ended, such as a Labor Day cookout or Fry-What-You-Want Party, you need to think more about the tangential guests—friends of friends, etc.—who have invited you to events in the past and might be hurt to know they were left off the list.** And don't forget those who live nearby. Sure, your next-door-neighbor may be annoying, but you know she's going to find out about the party when she sees all the cars in her driveway. And the

more people you invite, the less time you'll have to spend with her anyway. Sometimes it's easier—and always more polite—to extend the invite and hope she's busy that night.

> Just because you can lick a stamp and slap it onto an invitation doesn't mean you can whip up the world's greatest coq au vin. Be honest about your own culinary abilities and plan your menu (or have food brought in) accordingly. If you're asking others to bring something, make sure it's not something that will be a total inconvenience (custom-made omelets, for example), too expensive (lobster with a truffled caviar sauce), or beyond their culinary expertise. Ask only those folks you know would be happy to contribute—and make sure the entire meal doesn't rest on one dish (so if Susie's daughter comes down with the flu at the last minute, you're not left with pasta and no sauce). A potluck dinner can be a great way to save yourself a lot of time and work in preparing for a party, and allows your guests to contribute more than just great cocktail party conversation.

If you do get outside assistance with your food (we won't tell), don't dip your head in a bowl of flour and drip olive oil all over your apron in an attempt to pawn the dinner off as one cooked by your hands. People will appreciate the effort you've gone to to serve them some delicious delectables no matter where they came from, not talk about your inability to put out a plate of cheese and crackers in your own home.

RSVPs

One of the most critical pieces of info you can give as a host—or respond to as a guest—is an RSVP. If you're the invited guest, be sure to RSVP sooner rather than later. If you have the time to attend the party, you certainly have the time to call the host and let him know you'll be there with bells on.

> Whoever coined the phrase "children should be seen and not heard" may have very well written it in the midst of a cocktail party. As a host, you need to make a decision as to whether or not you want kids to be a part of the event. If yes, make that clear on the invitation— address it to The Phelps Family and even go so far as to say "the entire family is welcome." **If not, address it to just the intended invitees and maybe even make a joke about it, such as "Leave the kiddies at home and join us for an adults-only night of sparkling wine and conversation."**

> As a guest, what's the best way to respond to an RSVP? The invitation itself will tell you: a printed invitation will tell you how to RSVP (usually a phone number or e-mail address). E-vites have a built-in RSVP system, which can make life easy for both host and guest. If someone invites you verbally, it's fine to respond in the same manner—even if you had to take a couple of days to check your schedule. Hey, you're a popular gal!

Host with the Most

A relaxed host is the most welcoming host. It can be disconcerting to arrive to an event and encounter a host with rollers in her hair and twenty different items awaiting their turn in the oven. It may sound like a pipe dream, but always try to schedule sixty minutes to yourself before your guests arrive—take a bubble bath, take your time getting dressed, then plop yourself on the couch and savor a nice glass of wine before your hostess duties officially begin.

> If the occasion calls for it, arrange for some backup. Having someone to cook and/or serve the meal ensures you'll have time to have fun (and gives you someone to blame if the salmon is overdone). It also lessens the load after the guests leave, as hired help can clean up and wash dishes as the night progresses. Be sure to tip your caterers well for allowing you to dodge the duties of a domestic diva.

> When introducing guests, make like a dating game show host and include a few additional details other than the person's name. You don't have to note the person's turn-ons and turn-offs, but think about particular details about particular friends beforehand, so that you can help to ignite conversation between your guests and keep the conversation flowing even when you move on to the next guest. You never know—your little party could just inspire the next great love story.

> Regardless of how impeccable your party-planning skills are, chances that the entire night will go off without a snafu are slim to none. While you can't plan ahead for unforeseen accidents—a tray of food knocked onto your brand-new carpet or a blackened-turned-burnt steak—you can practice your "calm, cool, and collected" face. **Maintaining a sense of humor is the easiest way to make people feel at ease and to leave your home feeling as if they had a great time . . . even if they didn't get to eat.**

If you happen to forget someone's name as you're making introductions—your coworker's husband, for example—just be honest. "Wow. I've been talking all night and I am embarrassed to say that I've forgotten your name." It may be a bit embarrassing now, but it's better than having to avoid this poor guy all evening.

> If things start going awry, don't be embarrassed to ask your guests for a helping hand (though the most polite of the bunch will have offered already). From the guests' perspective, witnessing the host go into party-meltdown mode can be a helpless feeling; they'll be happy to assist and get the evening back on track as quickly as possible. "Joan, would you mind grabbing another bag of ice from the freezer? There's no better way to wash down an overcooked stuffed mushroom than with an ice-cold martini."

> If you are hosting a party and expect a number of kids to be in attendance, treat your guests to the luxury of a babysitter—one you hire to play games, color, or otherwise keep the gaggle of tots entertained and distracted while the adults mingle. Designate one area as the "kid zone" and keep them occupied there with plenty of movies, treats, and fun. Just make sure you don't place the kiddie drink table right next to the bar area.

> As a guest, don't ever assume that your own kids have been invited to a party. If you've been invited somewhere and exactly who the invitees are isn't clear, simply ask. The host will appreciate you clarifying ahead of time as opposed to showing up with your terrible-twosome twins in tow. If you are invited to an adult-only party and cannot find a babysitter for the night, you need to accept the fact that you're going to have to forgo the revelry and decline the offer. **Never ask a host to make an exception for you because you cannot get a babysitter.** It puts the host in an uncomfortable situation and could bother the other guests in attendance—both those who were looking forward to a kid-free night and those who might feel slighted that their own children weren't "invited."

Cleaning House

Cleaning house is probably the most important job a host has leading up to a party (well, that and a trip to the liquor store). If you can't find the time to do this on your own, consider calling in a service. Cobwebs and beer do *not* go together.

> Don't assume that the party will remain 100 percent contained to the areas you've selected. There may be people who have never been to your home and are looking for a tour. This becomes a much more difficult prospect when one bedroom is piled to the ceiling with toys and dirty laundry. Avoid any unwanted guests by locking the doors to those rooms you don't want them seeing—or be sure to have the house completely cleaned and ready for oohs and ahhs.

The Perfect Guest

It takes a good guest to know one. Getting invited to parties is simple: be well behaved and people will want to have you around.

> Someone else's home is probably never going to be as comfortable as your own—you would have decorated it differently or chosen a different menu. But there is never an excuse to complain or make comments about someone's home, menu, etc., as a visitor, even if the meal is basically inedible. Someone has opened the door of his home to you, which is about the highest social compliment you can get. Show your gratitude by keeping your mouth shut.

> Likewise, you're not likely to have an instant connection with all of the other folks in attendance. There's always that one person at a party who clearly wants to be the center of attention—who takes it upon herself to complain loudly about the food, or turns her attention to you and makes her opinions known for all the room to hear. Do not be sucked into this person's vortex of negativity—or let her instigate anything with you. Politely extricate yourself from the conversation without acknowledging her negative comments— "It was nice to meet you Joyce"—and move on to the next guest.

Always arrive on time, not even just five minutes early, as you're likely to catch the host running around doing a last-minute check of everything. The phrase "arrive casually late" really refers to about fifteen minutes late, which is an acceptable time to arrive at a party. Much later than that could be considered rude, particularly if it's a dinner party or something that the host needs to time. You don't want to be the one to blame for a hot meal turned cold.

Bearing Gifts

Whatever the occasion that brings you to someone's home, never arrive empty-handed. No, not even if the invitation states "No gifts." Always arrive with something for the host—a bottle of wine, a box of candy, a bouquet of fresh flowers—but always remember that this is a gift for the host, for her to use/display/eat/drink on her own terms. Don't force the gift onto the event itself, such as by offering to open the wine you brought. If the host wants to save the good stuff for herself, let her.

> If your plans change—even at the last minute—always call (don't send an e-mail, text, or carrier pigeon to) your host to convey your apologies for not being able to attend. Make sure your reason is legitimate. If you decided you just don't want to go, suck it up and attend if you said you would—you can always duck out early. Chances are you'll end up having a lot more fun than you expected.

Party Talk

No one wants to enter into a political debate between the cheese and dessert courses. Conversation should always be light and nonconfrontational. **Discussing current events or recent newsworthy topics is fine, but this is not a time to whip out your ACLU card and hold the rest of the party hostage to your political ideologies.**

> If there is a loaded adjective to describe your particular sense of humor—scatological, sophomoric, mean-spirited, or twisted—keep your attempts at levity more middle-of-the-road if you're meeting even just one person for the first time. You never know what sort of joke or conversation topic is going to offend or embarrass someone else, so keep your sarcasm to yourself, even if a few other guests aren't being so PC.

Menu Time

If you're playing chef at your own party, don't treat your guests as culinary guinea pigs. You want to make sure that the food is edible, so stick to tried-and-true recipes. Sound like a real chef by calling it your "signature dish."

> A good host always anticipates his guests' needs, including dietary ones. Be sure to ask people if they have any food allergies or dietary restrictions. Burgers and hot dogs on the grill may be a great meal for a casual barbecue—as long as you have a few alternative entrees on hand for the vegetarian in the group. (No, potato chips don't count as a protein.)

If you're opting to host a buffet meal, make sure you have enough seats and table surface for all your guests. Otherwise you could end up with a couch full of penne alla vodka and your best friend could end up with it on his shirt.

> If hosting a cocktail party, hire a bartender and keep it professional. It doesn't have to be expensive. The side benefit: she can keep an eye on alcohol consumption—and make sure there's plenty of coffee on hand. If your bar is serve-yourself, you should always have a nice selection of beer and wine available, but don't forget a couple of exciting beverages for the teetotalers in the crowd. Tap water can only garner so much excitement.

> As a guest, don't be the party-goer who mixes up the serving utensils while eating from the buffet. And keep in mind that this smorgasbord is for everyone—it is not your personal serving tray—so only use serving utensils to take your food. **Your fingers should never double as tongs.**

> If there is nothing to eat that suits your mood or dietary restrictions, don't talk about it—and don't head to the kitchen to whip yourself up a peanut butter and jelly sandwich. If your diet is limited by a medical condition such as diabetes, it's helpful to stow a snack bar or other edible tide-me-over in your pocket for these very sorts of occasions (just maybe sneak away to the bathroom or some other place to gobble it down). If your eating habits are more finicky than medical, do your best to eat what you can without drawing attention to the lack of food on your plate. You can always hit the drive-through on your way home.

The Extra Man

A party may be a great way to introduce the latest love of your life to your closest friends and family members, but never assume that an invitation is addressed to you *and* whomever you want to bring along.

> It's never polite to simply invite someone to come along with you to a party or to show up with an unannounced guest. If you've received a party invitation that is just for you, and your host is someone who can take a hint, you *can* mention something about the special someone you've been spending a lot of time with—"I can't wait for you to meet the new guy I've been dating. We'll have to meet up for a drink some time soon."—and hope that the host takes the bait. If she does, good for you. If not, make the decision as to whether you can bear the thought of a night away from your new love.

If you are the host and someone shows up with an unexpected guest in tow, do your best not to flinch. Make that person be it a cranky in-law or bratty kid feel welcome. Don't make a big deal about having to reconfigure the seating or add another table setting. You can drag another chair over without the loud sighing and eye rolls.

Happy Hour

Whether or not to serve alcohol—and in what varieties and quantities—is a decision that belongs to the host alone. If you have a specific reason for not wanting to serve alcohol, that is certainly your choice. But having at least one type of alcoholic beverage available—be it some beer or a nice bottle of wine—is always appreciated by guests.

> If you've opted not to serve alcohol at an event because there is a recovering alcoholic in your midst, don't take it upon yourself to announce this to each and every guest as they enter the front door. It's also not the host's responsibility to put a cap on how much food or drink any single guest is allowed. Simply set up your beverage buffet and leave it at that. Do not make it your job to monitor the intake of your guests or question who is, and is not, partaking.

Assigned Seating

It's the host's decision whether to have assigned seating or let the guests fall where they may. If you as host have a specific seating arrangement in mind—your inner Cupid just can't help himself—the easiest way to get your point across is with seating cards. Otherwise, a verbal rundown of who goes where is totally fine. Just make sure everyone is paying attention.

> If you've been invited to dinner and the host has chosen to arrange the seating herself, never try to pull one over on everyone and change your seating location. The host will surely know—and fume. And she probably had a reason for placing you there anyway . . . even if she has stuck you in between two of the night's biggest duds.

> If any youngsters have made the guest list, make sure there's something kid-friendly to eat. If you're the parent

of a finicky toddler, don't try to force new food on him to impress your friends. **If Junior's tastes run more toward peanut butter and jelly, bring that along for him; tonight is** not **the time to introduce him to liver pâté.**

CHAPTER 7

In Conversation

With the proliferation of new media technologies—e-mail, texting, IM, etc.—the way we communicate is constantly changing. Formal greetings seem to be going the way of the VCR, a trend worth reversing.

Greetings and Salutations

Saying "hello" is not always as easy as just that.

> > You may want to be seen as the "cool" mom or dad, but children should always be taught to refer to adults in a formal way—Mr. and Mrs. Wilson, not Brian and Julie. This formality begins with the first introduction. When you introduce yourself to a youngster, you do so as Mr. or Mrs. When you refer to other friends' parents, refer to them as "Mr." and "Mrs." too. Even if you *are* a fortysomething.

Cell Phone Social Graces

Not all that many years ago, a "mobile phone" was the size and weight of a six-month old baby—and only powered executives had them. As cell phone culture becomes ubiquitous, so does rudeness. The world has become our living room—a place to hunker down and have a chat, even one on the most private of topics.

> A ringing cell phone doesn't always have to be answered. Originally, cell phones were meant for doctors and the president—you know, people with really important jobs who might need to be reached at all hours of the day and corners of the earth. **Today, try finding a preschooler who isn't toting a BlackBerry in his SpongeBob lunchbox. Just because you** can **be reached everywhere doesn't mean you should be.**

> Whether you're meeting someone for a business or personal matter, you've scheduled the meeting for a reason and it's only fair to focus all your attention on that person. It would be easy to fill a book with a list of times and places where it's inappropriate to answer a cell phone (or return a text or e-mail), and most of them are obvious, dates, business lunches, and funerals being just a few of them.

> When meeting with others, if you're waiting on an urgent call, such as a family emergency, and absolutely cannot turn the phone off, make sure to set it to vibrate and let the others know—at the beginning of the meeting—that you apologize in advance but you're expecting an urgent call that you must answer. That way, if a call comes in during your meeting, they know ahead of time that it cannot be avoided. If the call does come in, leave the area and find a private place to speak—outside, in the lobby, etc. Restrooms aren't advisable.

You and your childhood chum's favorite New Kids on the Block song may make you laugh when it blasts each time she calls, but it can be ear-piercing to a stranger who doesn't know all the memories behind it. Assigned ringtones can be a great way for you to not have to turn your head to see who's calling, but be aware that ringtones become public property whenever your phone is set to anything other than vibrate. Obscenity-laden tracks to indicate your boss is on the line might not play well with the parent standing behind you in line at the grocery store.

> As rude as it may be for someone to force her private cell conversation on a room (or train) full of unwilling participants, you telling the person that she is being rude is just as inappropriate. Unless there are posted rules about cell phone use and who you can report the infraction to, like it or not, cell phone behavior is up to the caller alone.

> A call log can be a forgetful person's best friend—but it can be a strong temptation for wannabe spies, too. If you're a parent concerned about what your child is up to, it's acceptable to scroll through to make sure there's no suspicious activity. But that rule doesn't apply to your spouse's personal possessions. In the same way that you should feel comfortable calling whomever you choose from your own cell phone, your friends, family members, and significant others should have that same right. Snooping isn't sexy.

Letter Writing the Right Way

A text message may be easier, but there's something to be said—and something awfully classy—about a handwritten letter, hand-delivered by the good ol' USPS.

> Your parents probably taught you the importance of sending thank-you notes when you were a kid, and there's no reason those lessons need to go by the wayside today, even if e-mail *is* a lot easier. If someone does something nice for you—sends a gift, takes you out for a celebratory meal, helps you paint your bedroom, etc.—a short handwritten note to express your gratitude is an excellent way to say thanks.

> A handwritten note is still *the* best way to thank a potential employer for his or her time following an interview. To be sure that the letter doesn't reach the hiring manager a day after you've already been notified of another candidate being chosen for the position, have it addressed, stamped, and ready to be written out before you even enter the building. Then, on your way out, you can add a name ("Dear Andrew") and a couple of quick details ("I was thrilled to learn about your new website initiatives"), drop it in the nearest mailbox (to shorten the delivery time), and rest happy knowing that you have just taken part in a time-honored employment tradition—and one that still impresses hiring managers today. (Particularly *because* it's so easy to send an e-mail instead.)

> If you've taken the time to sit down and handwrite a letter, you should also take the time to use proper punctuation, grammar, and capitalization. Don't turn this into a handwritten text message—LOLs, emoticons, and all. **Respect the rules of the written word. Imagine that your ninth-grade English teacher will be checking your work.**

> In letter writing and electronic communications, it's important to remember that the written word does not always indicate the correct inflections. (No, not even if you underline or use italics.) Always be aware of how certain phrasing might be misconstrued and tweak your language accordingly. It's perfect acceptable—even recommended—that you write a "test" version of any letter before committing the real thing to paper. A letter received with a million cross-outs, erased phrases, and whiteout only causes the reader to wonder what you're *not* saying.

Internet Manners

In the good old days (a whole decade ago), people exchanged phone numbers as a way to keep in touch. Today, it's all about e-mail addresses and Facebook accounts. Even the smallest mom-and-pop shop seems to have a dedicated URL, which means communication between human beings has gone virtual in a previously unimaginable way. While the Web opens up a world of new people/places/things to learn about and connect with, it's also a place where poor manners run rampant.

The Internet gives anyone who wants it a public forum for his opinions. If you wouldn't openly espouse your beliefs to a room full of strangers with all eyes on you why take to a message board to do it? Just because you can say something "anonymously" online doesn't mean you should. Don't post anything online that you would not say directly to the target in question. No, not even public figures.

> When it comes to your own computer, go hog wild—set the font as large as you like and make sure that your computer collects cookies galore if you wish. But if you share a computer with someone else, or are borrowing someone's laptop for the weekend, do not change settings so that the preferences are yours. If you share a computer with someone, compromise—just as you would about which television programs you're going to watch or whether you're going to be skim or soymilk drinkers.

> To be a well-mannered web user, it's important to know the difference between the Internet as a tool and the web as entertainment. If you're given full Internet privileges at work, you should only engage in web surfing that is germane to the business at hand. There's never an excuse for playing around during work hours. A quick hand of solitaire never hurt anyone . . . except for getting people fired.

> Employers have every right to take whatever measures they deem necessary in order to ensure that work time is productive, not playful, even if transgressing employees *do* feel violated. This includes Internet usage. Hours logged at the office are the company's time—not yours. That computer you're using? The company's, not yours. **Make sure that any web surfing, etc. is all in the name of the your employer's bottom line—not your love life or some other personal endeavor.**

> The beauty of the Internet is that it allows you to connect with millions of people from around the world whom you likely never would have met otherwise. Being a regular visitor to certain websites or chat rooms can be a great way to "meet" people with similar interests. But just because you have similar interests doesn't always mean you'll be of the same opinion on matters. Just because you can hide behind the anonymity of your computer screen doesn't give you—or anyone else—the right to disrespect someone else's opinion. You may both be a part of the Baseball Fanatics chat room, but a Yankees fan and a Red Sox devotee are not always going to be the best of friends in this sort of setting.

> Dialoguing back and forth about your difference of opinion—providing a clear argument as to why you feel the way you do, with him responding in kind—is one of the things that makes the Internet so engaging. But screaming at each other (via all caps) and taking personal potshots at each other is no way to have a civilized disagreement or

conversation. This kind of behavior is known as "flaming" and is just as obnoxious to the other people who use the website as it is the victim of the attacks. If a person you've been communicating with online decides to escalate his attacks and behave in an inappropriate way, ignore him. Stop the communication in its tracks immediately and refuse to engage in this sort of back-and-forth. No, you don't even have to tell the person why you're stopping the conversation—that will only further enrage. He'll get the message soon enough and find another victim; the web is full of pent-up anger.

E-mail Etiquette

E-mail leaves what we like to call a "paper trail," meaning explicit proof of something you've said, done, or admitted to. It's admissible in a court of a law and certainly in the court of public opinion.

> Never send any confidential information via e-mail, such as credit card information or a social security number. And never forget how easy it is for someone else to forward your words (intentionally or otherwise) to someone else. Be careful about what you say about others in an e-mail conversation—even a friendly one. There are many ways for the person being discussed to get a hold of that correspondence. **Always expect the words you write in an e-mail to remain in existence for all eternity—and choose your words accordingly.**

> Just because the technology with which an e-mail is sent allows for a more expedient method of communication doesn't mean that the manner in which you write an e-mail should be relegated to shorthand. This is particularly important in business communication. Just because you're submitting a resume via e-mail doesn't mean you should ignore the normal rules of business correspondence. Sending a note in all caps or, perhaps even more annoyingly, all lowercase letters, without regard for appropriate grammar or punctuation, is not the way to put your most professional foot forward. But if a backward step is what you're seeking, by all means, proceed!

> The fine art of face-to-face (or even telephone) conversation seems to have been replaced by e-mails and instant messages. Always remember that, in the heat of the moment or a brutal argument, it's best not to play into the "I'm going to respond right away" game, as it generally only results in hurt feelings. If you and an acquaintance are engaging in a battle of words and wits via e-mail, have the courage—and prudence—to change the platform to in-person or voice-to-voice when things start to go a little too far. Vocal inflections and body language connote a lot more than words displayed on a cell phone screen ever can about intention and attitude. **Don't fall into the e-mail argument trap; not even OxiClean makes a solution powerful enough to clean up that mess.**

> Everyone has that one friend who constantly sends e-mails that are half emoticons and half real, English-language words. Whether you're the culprit or victim in this sort of crime against communication, it's important to keep these basic rules in mind regarding any sort of e-mail communication:

- ALL CAPS INDICATES THAT YOU ARE YELLING!
- all lowercase letters are just as offensive—particularly in business communications. and don't forget it, jack.
- You may be thrilled to hear you landed the job, but an emoticon is not the way to express that :-)
- Never presume that a first-name basis with someone is okay until he or she has told you otherwise. Outreach should always be made to Mr. or Mrs., never Dennis or Jacqueline.
- Be aware of your grammar and spelling. Always give any note a quick proofread before sending it out; a **typi** can be really embarrassing. And in business communications, it can be grounds for the recipient to not want to continue the relationship. (Yes, really.) Particularly when it comes to applying for a job, one typo can send your resume into the circular file—no matter how glowing your employment record may be otherwise.

> With e-mail so quick and easy—and available on just about every cell phone and portable device—it's quickly becoming *the* main method of communication for many people. Don't wear the fact that you haven't picked up a

telephone in more than a year as a badge of honor. Electronic communication may be convenient, but don't let it supersede phone calls and in-person meet-ups as your *only* form of communication. Believe it or not, there are plenty of people who want to hear your melodious voice and see your smiling face on occasion.

Just as the clothes you wear reflect a message about who you are, your e-mail address and screen name do the same in electronic communications. Your "Maddog" nickname may be a funny inside joke to friends and families, but could be off-putting to new acquaintances and potential business partners, particularly if you run a daycare center or a series of anger management classes. Stick to something simple like *your name*, perhaps

> Not having the time to properly spell-check or proofread an e-mail is never an excuse for not doing it. Think of it this way: if you don't have the time to proofread it, then you don't have the time to write it. Hold off until you have that extra 30 seconds to be a proper e-mail sender. Don't forget that electronic spell-checkers don't always pick up on every typo (especially if you've included some of those dreaded all-caps words). The last thing you want is a typo in your dressing-down of someone via e-mail.

Texting Tutorial

Keep in mind that not everyone likes to text, and not everyone has an unlimited texting plan on his cell phone. Which means aside from being an unwanted way for the recipient of your text messages to communicate, it could also be costing him dearly—literally—to do so.

> If you *must* text, resist the urge to channel your inner storyteller and send your message in ten separate messages of just a few words each. It doesn't create suspense or excitement on the part of the reader; it causes a headache from listening to the text alert ding again and again and again and again . . .

> At its heart, texting is really a way for you to invade someone's personal time and space with conversation. Just because you love to spend your Friday nights flirting with friends on your cell phone doesn't mean other people appreciate this. Don't forget how easy it is for the wrong person to read your text. Sure, it's downright rude to read text messages or review a call log that doesn't belong to you, but it happens, probably more often than you think. Do you really want to be the cause of strain in your friend's marriage because your playful message rubbed his wife the wrong way?

> Look at texting as a way to get a message to someone quickly and with little fuss. It's a great tool when there's too much noise to hear someone on the phone very well, but it's extremely casual in nature and is viewed that way. There

may be occasions where you find yourself texting with a work associate for one reason or another, but never allow a text dialogue to become a full-fledged business conversation. That sort of matter requires a more formal setting—meeting, conference call, or even an e-mail. Likewise, in your personal life, it's never okay to have a "serious" conversation over text—to deliver bad news ("I'm breaking up with you!") or even great news ("I'm pregnant!") in such an impersonal manner.

If you must text, consider your surroundings: Are you driving a car? Put the phone down! On a date? Put the phone down! Sitting down for a cup of coffee with that sorority sister you haven't seen since college? Put the phone down! Some people seem physically unable to leave their cell phones alone for more than 30 seconds at a time. Don't be the latest person to succumb to the CrackBerry. It's incredibly rude to the person you're with, and makes her feel unimportant and small. Do you really want to inflict that on someone just to make sure your picks for this week's fantasy football game get logged in time?

Social Networking Charms

For many people, the invention of Facebook seemed to spell the end of regular communication as we know it. And the list of people we refer to as "friends" is growing at an alarming rate. Social networking sites are a great way to keep the masses informed of your latest news (and, if you wish, your whereabouts), but should never take the place of personal conversations.

> Though social networking can be utilized for both professional and personal reasons, you don't have to mix the two if you don't want. There are two sides to every person: the at-work side and the at-home side. If you'd prefer not to witness those worlds colliding, it's perfectly acceptable to maintain different social networking accounts for these different purposes. For example, you could have a LinkedIn account for work matters and a Facebook account for friends, family, and long-lost grade school chums with whom you have virtually nothing in common.

> Never forget the viral nature of social networking sites. Your next-door neighbor may not be a friend, but she could have access to some of your postings through another, mutual friend. So before you start kvetching about the loud music coming from her backyard, be aware of who may be privy to your postings. Also: think about the light in which you're casting yourself before you post any sort of status update. Just because you're furious with your best friend today does not mean that will be the case tomorrow. **Never vent about your frustrations in a public forum, where it will live on in perpetuity.**

> Similarly, even if your posting is not at the expense of someone else, think about the message you're sending about yourself—and your own self-importance—before

you post. Does anyone *really* care that the tomatoes at the grocery store were not as red as you like them? Or that you're exhausted/happy/sad/bloated? Posting something to a social networking site is akin to wearing a sandwich board with the same message. Is it something you really think people need to know?

> Even if you *do* continue to play Howard Cosell and give a play-by-play of your hourly activities, not everyone in your circle of friends will be comfortable with that. Before you post dozens of photos from last weekend's costume party and identify each person in the photo, check with those folks you're planning to "tag" or caption to make sure they are okay with it. It doesn't matter whether the photo is compromising in any way or not. They all have the right to say how, when, and where—and whether— their likeness is used. This includes using it on a social networking site.

Politics as Usual

Political freedom is a constitutional right in the United States. But that doesn't mean that talking about politics with every Tom, Dick, Harry, and Barack isn't without potential faux pas.

> Politics is one area where people get easily heated; it's a topic where conversation can quickly turn into debate— or full-out fisticuffs. If you want to talk about your political viewpoints, join a group with shared interests or attend

a town hall meeting. **A cocktail party or other random meeting is** not **the place to talk about who you voted for and why, or how you think the country is going to hell.**

> If a friendly debate *does* turn into an all-out ideology war, the best course of action is to back off. Regardless of how passionate you may be about a topic—or how wrong you think your opponent is in his opinions—the moral high ground is always the best road to take. Tell your opponent that it's time you agree to disagree and move on (ideally to another partygoer). Differences of opinion are what make the world go 'round . . . and just a little bit crazy.

> Proud to be a member of a certain political party? Expressing your support silently—with a bumper sticker or campaign pin—is one way to show your support without getting in someone else's face. If you have a burning viewpoint that you're just dying to get off your chest, your weekly bridge game isn't the appropriate forum. How about a letter to the editor of your local newspaper instead? If printed, you've got a much larger audience than that pesky old PTA meeting could ever afford—and you've expressed yourself in a controlled, thoughtful, and intelligent manner, which is the only way to get a point across in the first place.

Constructive Criticism

Good manners aren't about keeping your mouth shut and always being agreeable. Sometimes it's about making your point—or disappointment—known, but doing so in a helpful, nonconfrontational way.

> When we feel we've been wronged in some way, the normal reaction is anger. Whether your own anger triggers rosy cheeks, a stern voice, or lots of talking with your hands, the fact that you are irritated should always be expressed through words alone, never actions. When expressing dismay, it's always necessary to take a deep breath and think before you speak. Figure out what part the person you're speaking with played in the problem—isn't the chef, not the waiter, the one who overcooked your steak?—and address that part specifically. If you express yourself clearly, calmly, and concisely, you're much more likely to get a positive response. Launching into a tirade only makes you seem like a lunatic—and makes the object of your attack less likely to want to work with you to resolve the problem. The phrase "Think before you speak" may be trite, but it's true.

> A great way to refrain from making a complaint personal is to forget that the words "you" and "your" exist and instead focus your language on making it a mutual problem—a mutual problem that you can fix together. Instead of yelling at your assistant that "You've screwed up the last three orders you've taken!" tell her that you know things have been very busy around the office lately and you're both overloaded at work. You want to make sure that she's able to perform to the best of her abilities, and you'd like her input on how you can best achieve

that—are there certain duties that are taking up more time than usual, etc. If you want to find a permanent solution to a problem, you've got to find at least a temporary way to curb your frustration and speak without anger.

> In many cases, the best way to lodge a complaint is in writing—whether in a letter or via e-mail. For people who dread confrontations, this can be a great way to show backbone, but it should be done with the utmost grace. Writing your complaint allows you to choose your words carefully; you should have a friend proofread the letter before you send it, lest you include phrasing that could be misinterpreted. Complaining in writing also has the benefit of letting you explain the situation a bit further. Written complaints should follow the same "forget the word 'you' exists" format as a verbal complaint. **Just as you would in person, you want to come across as calm, cool, and collected—which means no all-caps, underlines, exclamation points, or, even worse, whatever you call the exclamation point-question mark combo!?!**

> Every problem has a beginning, and if you're complaining about an ongoing issue, it's best to include a recap of the history of the problem. For example, if you purchased a new piece of furniture that—six months later—is still resting comfortably on the store's showroom floor, you'll want to provide the dates of all key communications with the company (when you purchased it and all follow-ups) as well as the people with whom you've spoken (always ask

for their names) and any written proof of these transactions/conversations (e.g., an original receipt or e-mail transcript). Don't think of your complaint as a vent session—it's your attempt to rectify a problem. And when you're the one who is initiating the complaint, it's up to you to propose a solution, such as: "As it's been a half-year since the furniture was originally purchased and promised for delivery, we have had to purchase another set and therefore request a full refund on the original amount of $2,500 within ten days of the receipt of this letter."

> In cases where you are providing a solution (or ultimatum), send the letter via some trackable format, such as certified mail, so that you can be sure of when the letter was received and by whom. If you set forth a time frame for follow-up in a letter and have heard nothing by the time your deadline has arrived (provided the given time frame is a week or more—not "32 seconds from receipt of the letter"), it's fine to follow up and inquire about the status of your complaint with a phone call, second letter, or in-person visit. But never get carried away in your persistence; there's a thin line between doggedness and harassment.

> If the matter still goes unresolved—and is the sort of problem where legal action must be taken—there's no rule that says you can't show class in the midst of a lawsuit. Regardless of how you've been wronged, it can benefit you personally, emotionally, and legally to act respectfully to all those you encounter, on your side and the opposing

team, throughout the entire legal ordeal. You never want to behave in such an obnoxious way that the other side just wants to stick it to you! If you're not the one who behaved badly in the first place, why start now?

CHAPTER 8

In Celebration

From religious events to family traditions, everyone celebrates holidays—if not the same holidays in the same way. But the rules of conduct during these celebratory events don't change too much from one person to the next.

Gift-Giving Basics

Birthdays. Christmas. Bastille Day. There are any number of occasions throughout the year where gift-giving becomes a mandatory sport. As with any sport, there are rules of the game in gift-giving. The most important rule: in any gift-giving scenario (with the exception of money or a gift card), always be sure to include a gift receipt with the item. That way, if it needs to be returned for any reason—damage, size, color, just plain wrong—there will be no hassles in doing so.

> If we bought gifts for everyone we know on every celebratory occasion, there'd be little money left to feed ourselves on a weekly basis. Therefore, the following "rules" are some standard practices when it comes to gift-giving:

- Birthday gifts to your own parents, siblings, and children are a lifelong responsibility.
- Other special children in your life should be given a birthday gift every year until they turn 18.
- Once a "child" turns 18, it's up to you whether you want to continue the tradition or only gift them on special-occasion years—21, the big 3-0, etc.
- If you're invited to a party—regardless of the person's age or how well you know him—you should always bring a gift. If the invitation says "no gifts," honor the host's wishes. If you really feel you must bring a gift anyway, make it something very small.

> Whether there's a special occasion or not, the one time where a gift is always required is when you're invited to someone's home. This doesn't need to be anything extravagant—a bottle of wine for a cocktail party, a kitchen gadget for a housewarming, a beach bag full of snacks and sunblock for a pool party—but you should never arrive at someone's home empty-handed. Unless you want this to be your first and only time on the host's guest list.

> For close friends, family members, and the young children of close friends and family members in particular, it's always polite to mark a special occasion—birthday, graduation, bar mitzvah, engagement—with a little something. Again, a gift never needs to be expensive. It may sound like a Hallmark card, but sometimes the nicest gifts are the ones that come from the heart and show how well you

know someone—a framed photo of the two of you, a copy of your favorite cookbook for a new homeowner, or a simple box of her favorite truffles. If you choose to simply acknowledge an occasion with a card, that's fine, too. But make sure it's a handwritten card—that will arrive before or on the big day—and not an animated e-card or posting on a social networking page to say "Happy B-Day!"

If you've been invited to a party to celebrate the special occasion, and that party happens to fall after the actual date, it's perfectly acceptable to bring the gift with you. In the event of a surprise party if you always *do* send a gift mail it ahead of time. It saves you the trouble of lugging the thing around all night and won't arouse any suspicion in the soon-to-be-surprised guest of honor.

> Just as we find it harder to select just the right gift for adult friends and family members as we get older, they're probably feeling the same way about buying for us. (The proverbial "what to buy the person who has everything" conundrum.) Kids, on the other hand, can be a snap. First off, they're always ready with a list of exactly what they'd like—and even if they're not so entrepreneurial (or don't have the ability of speech yet), it's easy enough to go into a store and find a great gift based on age. **If you're dying to get something special for that favorite nephew of yours—the drum set he's been asking for . . . or the pony—it's always best to check with a parent ahead of time.** You want to be sure that, first,

you are not duplicating a gift and, second, the parent is okay with the gift you are purchasing. (What's a kid going to do with *two* ponies?)

> One of the best resources for a purchasing a child's gift is another child. If you have access to a kid around the same age as the child you're buying for, by all means, treat her to a mall shopping trip and let her explain the ins and outs of all the newest toys and gadgets and help make you the coolest aunt on the planet this year. **No matter how much the kid tells you otherwise, though, explosives, pets, and liquor do** not **make great kid gifts.**

> We all remember that feeling of tearing through a pile of birthday presents . . . only to find a box filled with clothing! While it's rude of a child to make faces, groan, or exclaim "I hate clothes!" when face-to-face with such a fashion-forward gift, it doesn't hurt for the gift-giver to try and remember what it was like to be a kid celebrating your birthday. If you have the option of a toy versus a tie, opt for the former.

Gift-Receiving Basics

When it comes to receiving a gift, there are really only two things to remember: smile and say "Thank you." Yes, even if your great-grandmother has handed you a bag of combs as a Christmas gift, you need to act as if it's the greatest bag of combs you've ever received. (And as it's probably the *only* bag of combs you've ever received, you're not really lying.)

> Never feel strange about returning a gift. The gift-giver's intention was to show you he cared about you. Make sure you get something you like out of it. You don't need to shriek and run right out the door with the gift receipt in hand when you unwrap a package to unveil a velvet Elvis poster, but you should always exchange a gift for something that you'll actually use when possible. If you have no idea what store—or decade—a gift came from, donate it to charity and feel better about yourself.

It's never too early to start coaching your children on how to receive gifts graciously. While some kids tend to rip their gifts apart like a wild animal tearing into its dinner, teach yours that slow and steady prolongs the gift-giving extravaganza. Of course, people expect and enjoy seeing a child so excited to be opening a gift. It's just not as cute when that child is celebrating his 28th birthday.

> One sticky situation—especially when you're opening your gifts in a public forum—is getting two of the same gift. Frankly, this tends to be more embarrassing for the gift-giver than it is for the recipient. If you've been given two of the same gift, in the presence of both gifters, make sure to let each of them know how well they did in choosing the perfect gift: "Clearly, the two of you know me very well!" Two of the same gift that you hate is actually a great opportunity to get rid of them *both*. If either giver didn't include a receipt with the gift, simply ask her if she can send it so that you can exchange the "duplicate" gift.

"I'd love to get the matching glasses to go with the plate set!"

> One way to get rid of unwanted or duplicate gifts is the act of "regifting," or repackaging the unwanted/unneeded present to give to someone on your own gift list. While a convenient (and frugal) solution, regifting can be a tricky business—especially if you and the gift-giver run in the same social circles. In most cases, the most appropriate reaction is to let the gift-giver know of the duplicate gift and ask if they wouldn't mind if you returned it to the store. Asking permission—rather than demanding the receipt—is always a great way to approach this some-times awkward transaction. And if all else fails, there's always eBay.

> If you do decide to regift an item, make sure you under-stand the risk involved: if you're not 100 percent careful choosing whom you regift the item to, the original gift-giver could find out. (Or, heaven forbid, the regifted recipient could even regift it back to the original giver.) **Don't regift just because it's easy and saves you a couple of dol-lars; if you receive a gift that you don't like—or already have—and know that a friend would love it, then it's fine.** (Just make sure it has no remnants of the original wrapping or gift card)!

Getting What You Want

Nowadays, you can create a wish list—or registry—for just about every kind of occasion. But just because you *can* create a wish list, does it mean you should?

> Even in cases where a registry is acceptable—a wedding registry, for example—you should never include this information on any sort of personal invitation. Gifting is a voluntary process. The greatest gift that one could ever ask for—at a wedding, birthday party, or any other event—is the invited person's presence. Let that be enough. Still, don't look a gift salad bowl in the mouth!

> Kid's parties are one area where gifting is getting increasingly hard to keep up with. This provides a great teachable moment for your kids; when planning a birthday party, teach your kids that the gathering itself is the gift. You're going to be spoiling the little tyke with your own presents, so there's no need to send his friends' parents—who may not know you or your child all that well—on a wild goose chase for the perfect gift. Institute a "no gifts" policy or even a "homemade gifts only" rule for your parties. Better yet, if people persist in wanting to bring something, teach your child the importance of charity; talk about the different types of charities in your area with patients in need—children's hospitals, nursing homes, animal shelters—and choose an organization that your child would like to support. If people insist on bringing something, let them know that a dog toy or can of cat food for your child

to donate to the local animal shelter would be very much appreciated. But, truly, their presence is the present.

Cold Hard Cash

Cash: it's the ultimate gift. It matches everything in your wardrobe and can be anything you want it to be. But wanting cash and asking for it are two different problems, and only one of them has a solution. There are many special occasions—a graduation or wedding, for example—where the gift-giver knows that cash is the standard gift. And in most cases, this is what the guest of honor will receive. (Studies have shown that as many as 78 percent of wedding guests give cash.) But it's never appropriate to tell guests this—in writing, online, via pony express, or any other way.

> If you're in serious need of cash to help pay for that grand wedding you're throwing, a more polite way to get this message out to your guests is to let just a couple of your closest friends (best man, maid of honor) and family members (parents) know that if anyone asks for gift suggestions, they can say that cash would be appreciated. So that the request doesn't seem gauche (even coming from someone other than you), have them elaborate on what the cash might be used for—e.g., "As they're hoping to buy a home in the next six months, I know a cash gift would be very much appreciated" or "If you want to make it easy on yourself and give cash, they're taking off for their honeymoon to Australia the next day and I know that would surely come in handy!" It's hard to argue with that logic.

> Cash can also be explained as an appropriate gift in instances where a couple has lived together long enough to not really need too many of the typical wedding gift registry items, such as a toaster or blender. A couple can collect a lot of housewares when they've lived in sin for a decade. **Just make sure that whoever you designate as the resident bearer of cash news isn't going to say something like, "Well the happy bride and groom told me to tell anyone who asked that they want cold, hard cash—and lots of it!"**

Birthdays and Anniversaries

It's a very rare friend who remembers every birthday and anniversary—and it's a task that is not without its challenges. The key to remembering these important dates in people's lives is to have a cheat sheet, otherwise known as a calendar. Most e-mail programs have an accompanying calendar, which you can set to repeat from year to year. You can set an annual reminder a week or so before the big day to remind you of the upcoming date, so that you have enough time to grab a gift and card. But be sure that you take all the credit for that steel-trap memory!

> When it comes to other people's anniversaries, it's fine to acknowledge most of them with just a card, but it's always nice to mark a milestone anniversary. Tradition dictates several anniversary gift themes, depending on which anniversary you're celebrating:

1st anniversary: paper or a clock
2nd anniversary: cotton or china
3rd anniversary: leather, crystal, or glass
4th anniversary: fabric, fruit, flowers, or electrical appliances
5th anniversary: wood or silverware
6th anniversary: candy, iron, or wood
7th anniversary: wood, copper, or home office equipment/ desk sets
8th anniversary: electrical appliances, linen, lace, bronze, or pottery
9th anniversary: pottery, willow, or leather
10th anniversary: tin, aluminum, or diamonds
11th anniversary: steel or jewelry
12th anniversary: table linens, silk, or pearls
13th anniversary: lace or furs
14th anniversary: ivory or gold jewelry
15th anniversary: crystal, glassware, or watches
20th anniversary: china or platinum
25th anniversary: silver
30th anniversary: pearls or diamond jewelry
35th anniversary: coral or jade
40th anniversary: ruby or garnet
45th anniversary: sapphire
50th anniversary: gold
55th anniversary: emerald
60th anniversary: diamond
75th anniversary: diamond

> Does that mean that leather chaps are the perfect third anniversary gift? Not really—these are themes only, so take your inspiration from the traditional gifts. **The one anniversary you can never forget? Your own. Unless you don't mind sleeping in the dog house.**

Religious Events

It's easy for religious holidays such as Christmas and Easter to become more about presents and chocolate bunnies than religion. A great way to make sure the meaning of the day isn't lost on everyone is to create a holiday church tradition that will always remind the family of what the holiday is truly about.

> If you're planning a holiday celebration—a brunch, for example—keep in mind the typical times that people would go to church (usually, in the morning) and plan your event accordingly. You wouldn't want your frittatas to conflict with the Eucharist.

> When it comes to those adorable holiday characters, a child has the right to believe in Santa Claus and the rest of the gang for as long as he can. **Always keep in mind how magical the holidays are to a child when discussing Kris Kringle, etc. in front of any youngsters.** If you want to talk about where those gifts are really coming from, wait until you know without a doubt that the little one has had that conversation with his parents. Be particularly careful with kids who have become recently in-the-know about

traditional holiday legends; when you have "the talk" with one of your kids, make sure he understands that he's part of a very special club now—the first rule of which is "You don't talk about the very special club."

> Religious holidays are not celebrated exclusively by those of the religious persuasion. Inviting non-Jewish friends over for Passover Seder, for example, is a great way to share a meal—and an extra dose of culture—with friends. On occasions when you're invited to a religious celebration that you're not familiar with, the Internet can be a great friend to you in helping to understand the tradition, its history, and its meaning. If you've been invited to a Passover dinner and want to bring a gift, make sure that whatever you bring says "Kosher for Passover" on it. As preparation for the holiday, Jewish families need to remove all non-kosher items from their home. If you bring something non-kosher as a gift, they won't be able to bring it into the home until after the holidays. And there's nothing fun about that.

Gifts in the Workplace

Whether you employ a staff of two or are one employee amidst 10,000, figuring out when to buy gifts, and for which coworkers, can be a daunting task. But what you give to your coworkers can send a message to everyone else, and raise a red flag to others.

> In general, workplace gift-giving is private and discretionary, but if you choose to give small tokens of your appreciation to those around you on birthdays or the holidays, by all means do so. But be sure to do so with grace and keeping the following in mind. Alcohol is forbidden in many workplaces, so before you purchase the newest bottle of Beaujolais for your deskmate, you should check your company policy. You also want to steer clear of anything that could be seen as too "personal" or any sort of gag gift that leans toward the naughty. So what does that leave you? If your boss is an avid reader, how about a copy of that book you just read and know she'll love? Or perhaps a DVD of your favorite film that you'd like to share with your assistant? Better yet, wrap up something that she can share with the rest of the office (if she feels so inclined), such as a box of chocolates. Or let her pick her own gift with a gift certificate to her favorite restaurant or store. **A pair of boxer shorts emblazoned with "That's What She Said" may make your boss giggle, but could be taken the wrong way by his secretary.**

Some companies impose limits on how much employees can spend on gifts in the workplace. Before you make any sort of purchase, you should determine whether your employers have rules on this sort of thing and abide by them. The greatest gift you can give your boss, after all, is total company compliance.

The Holiday Season

The weeks between Thanksgiving and New Year's Day are typically party season. From a turkey dinner with the family until the ball drops on December 31st, there are many occasions to celebrate in the final weeks of the year, and even more manners to mind.

> At the busiest travel time of the year, traffic and crowds during Thanksgiving are as guaranteed a sight as the giant turkey in the Macy's Thanksgiving Day Parade. If your Turkey Day plans require traveling somewhere—by car, plane, bus, train, boat, or stagecoach—you need to anticipate that you're not going to have the road all to yourself. Steel yourself for this guarantee ahead of time and do your best to go with the flow. You all have the same goal in mind—arriving at your destination in one piece—so do your part to keep a positive attitude and maybe it will catch on.

> Sometimes the most annoying people you'll encounter during the holidays aren't the road-rage-afflicted other drivers or the argumentative couple seated next to you on the plane, but your very own flesh and blood once you arrive at your destination. Everyone seems to have that one family member who likes to drink too much, argue politics, or act like an all-around jackass at the Thanksgiving table. Chalk it up to family tradition; you'd miss it if he weren't there to uphold the custom.

> Like mashed potatoes and gravy, houseguests are a traditional part of any Thanksgiving dinner. Whether you are staying in a family member's guest room or opening every available couch and floor space to your own family members, you want to make sure the stay is a comfortable—and enjoyable—one for everybody. If you're hosting guests, the most generous thing you can do is to make sure that your guests have a clean place to stay—and one well-stocked with all the amenities they might need during their visit. This means making sure the guest room (couch, barn, or whatever) has had a good cleaning ahead of time, with clean sheets and comforters, dusted fixtures, and freshly swept/vacuumed floors. Bathroom essentials—toiletries, washcloths, and towels—should also be in full supply, and within easy reach.

> Think of some of the nicest hotels you've stayed at and do your best to replicate the experience in your own home for your guest. Keep some fresh water in the fridge and find out if there are any food preferences or restrictions that you should be aware of ahead of time. The days leading up to Thanksgiving can be stressful, but if you're having houseguests you need to make sure the pantry and fridge aren't marked as "Thanksgiving only." Make sure there are plenty of easy snacks (fruit, nuts) and easy-to-prepare meals (cereal for breakfast) that will make your guests feel at home and not leave them starving.

> As host, when someone asks what they can do to help, forget your control-freak tendencies and let them know. "Could you grab me that celery root from the fridge?" Even if it's a non-kitchen-related task—"Would you mind letting Fido outside for a few minutes?"—the guest you're slaving away in the kitchen for should be happy to help, and it's one of the few times where you can play queen for a day and have every wish granted. Just don't take it too far and ask them to polish your throne.

Back in the day, the women did the majority of the cooking and cleaning while the men sat in the living room watching football. Well, the rules have changed, friends. *Everyone* should offer to help in some way for Thanksgiving and keep offering to help as the opportunity arises. When you're invited for dinner, ask if there's anything you can bring. As you're getting ready to drive to the destination, call the host once more and ask if there is anything she needs; there's always that last-minute bag of ice or 20-pound turkey that might need to be picked up. When you arrive at your destination, find out what you can do to help: set the table for dinner or clear it once dinner has been consumed.

> Two of the year's biggest holidays—Hanukkah and Christmas—have a similar tradition: lights. **In either case, you should feel free to decorate your home for the holidays in whatever way you see fit, but keeping in mind**

the aesthetic value of the neighborhood and the line between tasteful and tacky.

> Many people drive themselves crazy each year trying to pick out the perfect gift for their loved ones. If you happen to stumble upon a cache of holiday gifts—mistakenly or otherwise—do not let the gift-giver know about the incident. Seeing the look on someone's face when she opens a gift you've spent time choosing for her is one of the real joys of the holiday season, so give the gift-giver a return on his investment. Don't let on that you know what you're getting, and, whatever you do, don't start using it.

> If you have a friend or family member who celebrates a holiday that is foreign to you—be it Christmas, Hanukkah, Rosh Hashanah, or Kwanzaa—take the time to do a little research and determine what the holiday is about so that you can ensure you don't behave in a way that is offensive to him or anathema to the holiday spirit (such as chowing down on a burger and fries while your friend is fasting for Yom Kippur).

CHAPTER 9

In Love

All you need is love. Love is a many-splendored thing. I will always love you. The phenomenon of love has been explored by artists through the ages—in art, song, movies, and literature. But experiencing it in life is a totally different ball game. Love can make us do crazy things, or so the saying goes. But it's important to make sure that "crazy" and "impolite" don't become interchangeable.

First Dates

If you're on the lookout for that special someone, the best way to meet someone is to let go of the inhibitions that might be holding you back. This could mean letting that cute guy at the other end of the bar buy you a drink or just becoming more open to meeting more people with varying interests.

> One way to meet new people is to do more yourself. Join in more social activities, say yes to every dinner party to which you are invited, or let your friends know that if they think of anyone you might hit it off with, you're game for grabbing a cup of coffee with him. Just be sure that the activities you're engaging in—joining a

ski trip club, for example—are something that you truly enjoy doing. Otherwise, the relationship will start off on a dishonest foot (and you could be saying your "I dos" atop the bunny hill).

> **While a woman making the first move used to be frowned upon, nowadays it's perfectly acceptable for a woman to ask a man out on a date.** Sometimes a guy might be too shy to make the first move—or afraid that the woman is going to say no. And many men find it refreshing to be asked out by a woman, since this takes some of the pressure off of them. Whoever is doing the asking, it's a question that should be done either in person or over the phone. Sure, it's easier to risk the rejection via e-mail or text message, but it's also very easy to misconstrue the question (or answer) via electronic communication. And who wants to risk that with a question this important?

> A series of flirtatious e-mails may lead up to one party telling the other about a great old movie playing at the revival theater this weekend. "I'm planning to see it again on Saturday night. If you're around, you're more than welcome to come." It might sound like an invitation for a date on the part of the person asking, but the recipient could just see it as a friendly invitation. Accordingly, she could respond negatively, "Sounds like fun, but I'm busy cleaning out my sock drawer that night" and dissuade the person from ever asking again. At the same time, the recipient may take it as just a friendly gesture and—with no romantic

feelings toward the other party—accept the offer without understanding the true intention behind the question. **Asking someone out, either in-person or on the phone, allows for intonation and body language, two important keys in revealing your true feelings.**

> An invitation for a date should be very clear-cut: "Would you like to have dinner with me on Friday night?" This allows the person to respond to the actual question being asked and the intentions with which the query arrives. So that there's no misunderstanding that you are interested in this person and are asking her out on a date, stay away from the more indirect—or deceitful—attempts to get someone to go out with you . . . especially if you've set the other person up to fail. "Jerry Seinfeld did *not* have his own television show in the 1990s! But if you're right, I'll have to take you out to dinner this weekend."

> If you are not interested in a person in a girlfriend-boyfriend kind of way, you owe it to him or her to be upfront—but kind—about it. But never forget that some of the greatest romances in history didn't start off in a fairy-tale way. If you enjoy this person's company and can see yourself being friends, why not spend an evening together and see if romance might be in the cards, too? If the spark isn't there on date one, you'll likely both realize it, making the opportunity to become friends over lovers a lot easier. Chemistry is a collaborative science.

> If you're the date-asker, it's up to you to plan—and pay—for the date. While you may want to impress this future spouse of yours, it's easy to go way over the top, which can be off-putting to your date. Being whisked away to Venice for a true Italian meal is certainly exciting, but also a bit overwhelming when coming from someone you've just met. It's not a bad idea to ask your date whether there's anything she'd like to do or a particular restaurant that she loves or has wanted to try. **You'd hate to find out that your date is a vegan only after you'd been seated at a prime table at MoMo's Famous Meat-Only Buffet.**

> A first date is about impressing your date, sure. But it's best to impress her with your good manners, wit, and charm—not the fact that you can drop $1,000 on a dinner. There is certainly a place for wildly extravagant dates in any romance, but those are for milestone moments. A first date should be somewhere comfortable, where you can focus on the business at hand: getting to know each other enough to determine whether a second date is in the cards.

> Dinner may seem a cliché first date, but it's a popular choice for a reason: we've all got to eat, after all. Plus, it's an opportunity to sit somewhere quietly and simply talk. And if the conversation is nonexistent, you've got a basket full of dinner rolls to stuff your face with until the check arrives. Food provides a distraction from a stilted conversation. Just don't let that distraction include a large piece of lettuce stuck in your front teeth.

If you are planning to pick up your date, make sure you've taken the time to clean your car out. The last thing she needs is to sit on a bag of fast food when she makes her grand entrance. When you arrive to pick up the date, always go to the door; never use your horn or just sit outside and wait as a way to "announce" your arrival. If your date lives with anyone—parents, a roommate, an exuberant pooch—you should meet each of them and say hello. Half of her opinion of you is going to rely on their first impressions anyway. (You get extra chivalry points for opening her car door throughout the evening.)

> Saying goodnight can be one of the most awkward parts of the date. You may wonder whether you should go in for a kiss or make plans for a second meet-up. Just as you put yourself out there to invite this person out in the first place, if you feel as if you'd like to offer a goodnight kiss or make plans for a second date, go for it. You'll learn quickly enough if the feelings are reciprocated.

> If the night went really well and you'd like to spend more time together, it's fine to ask your date if she'd like to continue the date with a nightcap, but this should be done as you're finishing up dinner and ideally in a public place. As much as you might want the night to never end, don't insist that your date invite you into her home or that she come back to your place with you. Wanting more of your date's company is the best way to end a night.

> If it's time to say goodnight and you realize there's no chemistry here, an easy way to communicate that—without hurting anyone's feelings—is to offer a friendly handshake and thank the person for a nice evening. If your date pushes as to when you might meet up again, it's best to stop that expectation in its tracks. "I had a great time but think we'd be better off as friends" is commonly understood as "I don't want to see you again." It may feel awkward to lay that kind of line on someone, but it helps to eliminate any hurt feelings. Sure, it may sting this person a bit tonight, especially if she thought the date went well, but in the morning, it's likely to be a forgotten scenario altogether.

> The end of the date is the best time to make your intentions known: if you'd like to see the person again, try and set up a date that night with a simple "I'd love to do this again. Would you be interested in getting together again next Friday?" If he responds positively, let him know you'll call him the next day (or whenever) to firm up the plans. Resist the urge to make it easy on yourself by scheduling a second date with someone with whom you are not interested romantically. You don't want to lead someone on or—worse—plan for something tonight only so you can cancel on him tomorrow. **Honesty is a dish best served immediately.**

Commitment City

There are few more exciting times in a relationship than the very beginning. It's the one time in the relationship where all those little quirks (which are bound to annoy you after twenty years of marriage) seem adorable and charming. But there are many ways in which to sully this getting-to-know-you phase.

> At some point in a relationship—one that is going well, at least—you and your smitten one will likely make the decision to "be exclusive" (or as they used to say, "go steady"). Basically, you've decided to invest your romantic energy into this one and only person and see where the love might take you. As this isn't the 1950s, you're not likely to get an ID bracelet out of it and no one is going to throw you a Monogamy Party. But making this commitment does take you one step forward in your relationship.

> The longer you date, the less formal the rules of dating need to be. For example, while some people like to adhere to "the man always pays" rule, long-term relationships are all about shared responsibilities, which include paying for dinners out and other activities. In some relationships, it's a tit-for-tat sort of situation—he paid for dinner last time, so you pay for it this time. You know you're in a meaningful relationship when no one seems to be keeping count. **If your beau of two months asks you to fork over an extra $3 because you ordered cheese on your hamburger, he's not a carnivore worth keeping.**

> If you are in a relationship with someone who likes to keep active—you're always eating out, going to the movies, taking vacations, etc.—and you're not able to keep up financially, it's best to address the problem sooner rather than later. **Let your significant other know that you enjoy the excitement of always being on the go, but that your checkbook isn't so happy about it.** Rather than suggest that he foot the bill for all of these luxuries, why not suggest that you make a concerted effort to spend a little more time at home or engaging in activities that don't cost a lot—and then take the initiative to make some plans, such as a picnic in the park, a home-cooked meal at your place, or a horror movie marathon with all the popcorn you can eat.

Online Dating

If you listen to what the commercials for the top online dating sites tell you, you can believe that one out of every five relationships begins online. Whether it begins in a virtual world or not, all relationships eventually move into the real world.

> Think of creating your profile as ordering off a menu: not only are you getting the chance to put all of the facts about who you are and what you are looking for out there for all the world to see (which hopefully means that only those who share those goals will reply), but you're also setting yourself up to find that perfect match. In essence, you're

creating an advertisement for what you're looking for in a life partner. Only soul mates need apply!

As with any relationship, the cardinal rule of Internet wooing is: be honest. It's fine to sift through box upon box of photos until you choose the one that catches you in just the right light . . . but it's not okay to post a photo from your high school prom if this year marks your 20th high school reunion.

> Don't forget that there are real people—and real feelings—behind the computer screen. As in real life, don't lead a potential paramour on if you have no interest in kindling a romantic relationship. If you have corresponded with someone a bit and/or met in person, then it's not okay to just ignore an e-mail. Again, honesty is the best policy: simply—and gently—let the person know that you have enjoyed getting to know him but that you don't feel a romantic connection. If you receive a note from someone via an online dating site and determine right away that it's not a love match—for whatever reason—don't feel obligated to respond. It will be less hurtful than responding simply to decline the offer to get to know each other better. By the same token, don't expect that everyone you reach out to directly will get back to you. Remember, this is all about making a match—and if someone doesn't see what a catch you are from your profile, there's no point in trying to persuade him otherwise. It's his loss!

> Think of each e-mail correspondence as a phone call: wait too long to send one, and you could be (wrongfully) signaling disinterest to the other party. Send too many—and make them too long or too personal off the bat—and you'll seem a little too intense. **Just as you wouldn't launch into your warts-and-all life story on a first date, don't be too revealing about your life in your early correspondence.** Keep your initial e-mails short, light, and fun—get to know who this person is and how he communicates as you lead into the bigger questions about life. Most important: keep it interesting. Make it a true reflection of your personality.

Be careful of choosing a screen name: you don't want to send the wrong impression. Even if party planning is your profession, partygirl2011 may send the wrong signal. A user name is the equivalent of your clothing in the online world: it tells the world about who you are and what you want.

> Create a separate e-mail address for online dating sites. That way, when you find Mr. Right, you can easily disable those accounts and not have to think about entering the dating pool again. It also helps from a privacy standpoint; people can't track you down using your e-mail address via social networking sites or a good old-fashioned Google search.

Breaking Up

When you break it down by the numbers, you only ever need one romantic relationship to work out. While you probably begin every relationship with the hope that it will lead somewhere, sometimes you just know that it's not right and the time has come to end it. That realization could come after a month, a year, a decade, or even longer. Regardless of how long you've been with someone, breaking up *is* hard to do.

> All relationships—with friends and enemies—are based on communication. If you enjoyed someone's company at one point enough to want to spend additional time with her, then you owe her the respect of actually discussing what you interpret as the end of your relationship. And you should have that conversation in person. **Dropping off the face of the planet or never returning another phone call is not a fair or respectful way to let someone know you no longer care to be a part of her life.**

> Just because you're the one who initiates the breakup doesn't mean that it's necessarily the other person's fault. Maybe you've been going through some changes in life—personal, professional, emotional—and just don't feel that you can be a good companion to anyone at the moment. Perhaps you've just decided that this whole monogamy thing isn't for you after all. Or maybe it's become apparent that your goals and those of your romantic partner are too different for you to succeed as

a couple in the long-term (he wants kids, you do not). It could be that you simply don't look forward to spending time with this person anymore. Whatever the reason, the person deserves an honest explanation as to why you don't think the relationship will work. And don't try the old "I've been selected to be a part of the next Biosphere project" line as an excuse. How many people are down there, anyway?

> One caveat about that whole honesty thing: if the issue is something that cannot be helped by the other person and could hurt her feelings if explained, a little white lie is not such a bad thing. Take an ear-piercing cackle, for example. It may have been cute the first time you heard it, but after a few months you've decided enough is enough. Let the person down gently; let her know that you've had a great time getting to know her but just don't feel as if the relationship is going to go much further and so you'd rather end it now as friends. Then brace yourself for the response.

> Breaking up can feel like a ton of bricks being lifted off your shoulders—or hitting you smack dab in the kisser. Getting dumped can hurt, and can trigger a defense response that leans toward the vengeful side. **Just because the woman you thought you would marry has just told you she no longer wants to see you doesn't mean you have the right to turn her life into a living hell.** The more calm and logical you are in dealing with a breakup, the quicker the pain will subside and you can move on. Just because

you know your ex's e-mail password and voicemail code doesn't mean you should immediately start concocting ways to use them to hurt her. Take a night to sleep on everything and see how you feel in the morning. Wanting to hurt that person the way she hurt you can be a natural response, but it's not something you should act on. You're better than that, right? *Right?*

PDA

On the opposite side of the "breaking up" spectrum are those couples who just don't seem to understand the difference between being affectionate with each other and needing a censor. Whether it's a couple of teens at the mall, your best friend and her new beau, your boss and his wife, or your grandparents, watching people cross the line of appropriate romantic behavior in public can be a disturbing sight. **If you've had the phrase "Get a room!" hurled in your direction on more than one occasion, that's a pretty good indication that you don't know the line between public decency and private affairs.**

> Sure, we all like to see two people in love—but affection can be easily displayed in the way that two people look at each other, speak with each other, help each other, and speak about each other in the other one's absence. Maybe your love can't be contained. But when you're in public—amid strangers or friends and family—the only appropriate public displays of affection are holding hands, putting your arms around each other, and nonlingering hugs or kisses.

Sticking your tongue down your boyfriend's throat only proves that you should have been left off of the evening's guest list—which is exactly what's going to happen the next time.

> What to do when you're on the observational side of an inappropriate lovefest between friends or family members? If you *truly* want to get the point across—particularly if there are young kids in the vicinity and you believe the behavior is inappropriate for them to witness—you'll need to take one or both of the offending parties aside (preferably the one you are closest to) and be honest that their behavior is making you a bit uncomfortable. You're pleased that the two have found each other and seem so happy together, but would they mind bringing the groping down a notch. There are kids in the room, after all. The couple in question is likely to react in one of two ways: embarrassment, with the promise that they will keep their love in check for the remainder of the evening, or anger that you've asked them to hide their affection (in which case they'll likely leave, so either way you've achieved your goal).

CHAPTER 10

In Marriage

Love and marriage go together . . . well, you know how the song goes, right? A wedding is a joyous occasion, but it requires a fair amount of decorum at every step of the way. By staying current with the latest thinking, you can bypass avoidable blunders and walk down the aisle with your etiquette in tact.

The Proposal

". . . And then he got down on one knee and asked me to marry him!" However the engagement story begins, if the answer is yes, then it ends in the same way: an excited announcement to friends and family that you and your loved one will be tying the knot. News of an engagement is one of the happiest announcements anyone will ever make in his or her life. And whether you're the one getting ready to walk down the aisle or it's a loved one, there are certain dos and don'ts pertaining to celebrating the happy occasion.

> While written announcements are no longer necessary— there are much faster and easier ways to get the word out—if you and/or your parents would like to announce the

happy occasion the old-fashioned way, it's up to you how fancy you want to get. A simple note printed out on your trusty printer, to be sent to friends, family, and perhaps the local newspaper, is one way to do it; formal stationary is the more traditional way to make the announcement. Typically, the engagement announcement should come from the bride-to-be's parents; if her parents are divorced, her mother makes the announcement, with mention of the father; if both parents are deceased, then a close family member—a grandparent or a sibling, perhaps—can be the lucky news-bearer.

While your recent engagement may be the biggest news in the world to you right now, it isn't the only thing on everyone else's mind. Don't be offended if people don't react in as ecstatically happy a way as you had imagined. If you're expecting Grammy to land a double back handspring upon hearing the news, you're bound to be disappointed.

> When you've received word that someone you know has gotten engaged, it's always nice to send a card congratulating the happy couple. It's up to you whether you want to send a gift as well; a wedding is one of those events where there's an awful lot of gift-giving happening—engagement gift, shower gift, wedding gift. If it's someone very close to you, a small token of your excitement—a subscription to a bridal magazine or bottle of bubbly—is always a sweet (and probably much needed) gesture.

> Just like the engagement announcement, an engagement party has traditionally been the domain of the bride's parents. But like many wedding traditions, this one is changing, too, given that so many of today's weddings are geographically diverse affairs with guests coming from all over the globe to attend. As such, one engagement or pre-wedding party isn't always enough. Today, a couple may have a series of pre-wedding events—engagement parties, showers—at a few key locations where multiple guests can attend. Which means it's not only parents who throw these soirees, but friends and other family members, too. Whoever is throwing the party (it should *always* be hosted; a bride and groom should never throw their own engagement fete) and wherever it is happening, it should be a low-key affair—an intimate cocktail party, a relaxed Sunday brunch, etc. It's a chance for people to express their congratulations to the couple in person, but it doesn't need to be a weekend-long affair.

> Though some guests are going to ask about where the couple has registered, as with any other invitation, registry information should never be volunteered. **If your goal in having an engagement party is gifts—not goodwill— you may want to skip the party altogether and rethink why you're getting married in the first place.**

> An invitation to an engagement party is like a pre-invitation to the wedding. Don't use an engagement party as a way to make those on-the-fence friends you're not sure you'll be inviting to the wedding feel better. Inviting someone to an

engagement party but not the actual wedding will only create hurt feelings and questions of "What the heck did I do wrong?"

> Don't forget that for every gift you receive you must write a thank-you note right away. So the more gifts you get, the closer you get to full-blown carpal tunnel syndrome. **A gift is a voluntary act of kindness; a thank-you note is not. Plenty of relationships have soured over this faux pas.**

> If you're getting married, you *will* need to register at some point in the process. For the couple who has never lived together, this can be an excellent opportunity to have friends and family help furnish your future home with vases and kitchen gadgets galore. Just be sure to register for a variety of items in a number of price ranges. You never know what someone can afford; if they're at least able to purchase you the one dish towel they know you wanted, they'll feel better about the smaller gift. Though wedding gifts are standard, never forget the reason you're having a wedding—for your loved ones to share in the joy of this special day. That's it. So if the only gift they can give you is their presence at the wedding (which, for those who are traveling from far away, can be an expensive prospect indeed), that should be more than enough.

> For couples who have lived together for a while, the registration process can be a bit trickier, as you likely don't need as much. But a wedding is still a new beginning for any couple. So if you're sleeping in a queen-sized bed now

but are planning to upgrade to a king at some point, it's perfectly fine to register for those items that you will want and need sometime down the road (e.g., bigger sheets). Your current apartment may be the size of a shoebox, but when you move into the place with the 1,000-square foot kitchen you've always dreamed of, think of the items you'll need to furnish it.

> Because some of your guests will still prefer to purchase gifts the old-fashioned way—driving to the store and paying for it there—be sure to register at a couple of different places that are easy for most to find. You'd be surprised how many retailers offer gift registries nowadays—from that tiny little frame shop around the corner to the biggest discount retailers on the planet. **Register at two or three different stores that offer something for everyone in terms of price range. Your guests will thank you for it.**

> An easy way to keep your guests apprised of information about the wedding is to put up a website dedicated to the big event. Whereas it's gauche to include any mention of gift registries on your wedding invite, it's acceptable to include this on a website. However, even if this is the main reason you created the website, don't simply broadcast that and leave the rest of the wedding details blank. If you're going to set up a wedding website, take the time to do it right, posting pictures and information about the engagement and the upcoming nuptials. Keep all of the information—including how you met and how he proposed—G-rated, of course. (Okay, we'll give you PG.)

> One important piece of information to include on any wedding website—as it's something that guests feel the most stress about—is dress code. But before you dictate what others should wear, consider the date, location, and time of the ceremony. Just because you've always dreamed of a Hollywood-style wedding does not mean it's fair to impose a black-tie affair on your guests. Before you choose your dress code, make sure that *you* understand what it means and that it matches your vision—and venue. Country club casual may make sense to you, but you should always include examples of what would be appropriate attire for both men and women in attendance. **A Friday afternoon wedding at your favorite Irish pub does not a formal affair make . . . though a tuxedo T-shirt might be appropriate.**

> Of course, not every engaged couple actually makes it down the aisle. There are a variety of reasons why a couple may choose to cancel or postpone a wedding. If you and your would-be-spouse decide to postpone your wedding or not to marry at all, you *must* return every gift you have received with a note thanking the sender but informing her that the engagement has been called off. An explanation is not necessary, but it helps put an end to any unneeded speculation and gossip. Of course, you don't need to go into the intimate details of what happened, how you made the decision, and what you were wearing when you threw the ring back in your fiancé's face, but a simple explanation at the ready to give those who ask (and one that designated close friends and family members can also share) will save

you both a lot of undue stress and embarrassment. If your wedding was called off as a result of untoward behavior on the part of either party, it's not the scorned lover's opportunity to drag his or her ex's name through the mud. Decorum goes a long way in taking the sting out of even the most painful situations,

Big Day Details

If the guest list is the most important part of the day—you really want your grandparents, siblings, nieces, nephews, and closest friends all there with you—take a moment before signing that deposit check to make sure you're choosing a place and time that most of your guests can manage; otherwise you risk them being absent from the proceedings. If your older relatives will have trouble making the trip to your desired location, or some friends might have trouble affording the travel costs of a destination wedding, maybe it's time to change the plan. You can choose a location you love in a place that is convenient for the majority of your most important guests, and save that hidden-away beach in Turks and Caicos you've been dreaming about since you were a little girl for the honeymoon. **In the end, it's totally up to you—but you're also not allowed to pout, be angry, or throw a fit when some of the invitations come back with regrets.**

> Always consider the ramifications of the time of year you want for your wedding, too. Winter white may be your color and a Christmas Eve wedding may be what you've always dreamed of, but you cannot expect that everyone you invite will be willing—or able—to abandon their families in order to attend your nuptials. Bah humbug!

On the List

At the same time you're zeroing in on the perfect location, you and your fiancé—as well as both sets of parents, if they are involved—should be whittling down the guest list to an appropriate number. **While tradition states that a bride's parents pay for the wedding ceremony and reception, there are no rules when it comes to who pays today.** With couples getting married later in life—many after having spent several years living together—it could be the couple themselves who pay, the bride's parents, the groom's parents, or a combination of all three.

> If your budget or location limits the number of people you can invite, and you're truly at a standstill in terms of negotiating whether his third cousin needs to bring a guest or your sister's boyfriend's dog-walker *really* needs to attend, take a few days away from the task to think it over. And if you simply cannot come to an agreement on who is coming and whom to leave off, it's best to let whoever is paying for the wedding cast the deciding vote.

Whether or not Mom and Dad are footing the bill, it is customary to work with them on the guest list. There are politics to be played when it comes to who gets an invite and who does not, and your parents may have good reason for insisting you keep or drop someone from the guest list. Hear everyone out before you start finalizing the head count. For the most part, 50 percent of the guest list should belong to the bride and the other 50 percent the groom. These numbers aren't exact, of course; when an only-child bride marries one of twenty-one kids, there's likely to be a certain amount of skewing but the guest list should never be a source of anger or stress. (Which is easier said than done.)

> Many wedding planners will tell you to assume that 10 percent of your guests will decline the invitation, but don't ever count on that as guaranteed. If your venue can only hold 90 people, you shouldn't invite 100, hoping that that 10 percent rule plays out in your favor. As a compromise on desired guests who simply cannot be accommodated, some couples like to designate an A Team—the friends and family whom you absolutely want to be there—and the B Team—those folks whom you'd love to see, but if space is an issue must be dropped. This can be a slippery slope, especially if members of the B Team associate with the A Team or are privy to any of your wedding planning details. You don't want your B Team neighbor to pick up your mail while you're away for a week and discover

that you're receiving RSVP returns when she hasn't even received an invitation.

> Whether you choose to invite someone from the get-go, or later on as you see how the guest list is playing out, anyone you are inviting to your wedding should receive a printed invitation—without exception (yes, even your parents, the best man, and the maid of honor). You may not need their RSVP card back to know that they'll be in attendance, but you need to send an invite anyway. If, as the RSVP date nears, you realize that your decline rate is much higher than expected, with a quarter of your invited guests saying they are busy that weekend, the only way to invite more people is with a printed invitation. If you do not have enough invitations to go around, you need to order more or shrink the guest list. An "invited" guest—B Team or even C Team—should never receive their invitation in-person, by phone, or—even worse—by word of mouth through someone else.

RSVP

As an invited wedding guest, you've only got two things to worry about as a loved one's wedding approaches: getting your response card back on time and choosing whether you want the lobster or filet mignon. There's no reason *not* to send the response card back—the invitation included a self-addressed stamped envelope, after all.

> The soon-to-be-wed have bigger problems to worry about than whether or not you'll be attending. So as soon as you receive your invitation—even if you've got weeks until the reservation deadline—send your response back. **You don't want to be on that list of wayward friends and family members who the bride and groom are forced to call for verbal attendance confirmations. They've got seating charts to fight over, after all.**

Party Time

Obviously the bride and groom are the guests of honor at a wedding, but when planning nuptials you can't ignore the fact that other people are thrown into the mix: your attendants. No one says you *have* to have a maid of honor or best man, nor are there any rules when it comes to whom and how many attendants you have.

> If you've been asked to play the part of attendant in a wedding, you should consider yourself the bride or groom's personal assistant up until they wave goodbye en route to their honeymoon. Depending on the people, this can be a thankless job at times. Just remember that planning a wedding is an extremely stressful and emotional time, and cut your friend a little slack if she seems a bit snippier than normal. Pulling your friend aside to address her bad behavior may make you feel better, but could further strain relations leading up to the big day (the bride already feels as if everyone is asking too much of her). Put your friend's feelings first and work to be the best personal assistant ever.

> If it's financially feasible, it's a wonderful gesture for the bride and groom to pay for the clothing their attendants will wear—the bridesmaids' dresses and tuxedo rentals. As it's unlikely the bridesmaids will ever wear their dress again, and each will be paying for a gift, the bridal shower, etc.—it can be a great way to show your appreciation for all these girls are putting in (financially and otherwise). If you can't afford to pay for your bridesmaids' dresses but would like to try and choose something that will make all of them feel comfortable, many new brides are simply choosing a dress color—even a simple black dress—and letting their bridesmaids choose their own styles. That way, the bridesmaids might be able to pull something from their already overstuffed closets, or at least choose something in their specific budget range, that makes them feel beautiful *and* that they'll be able to wear again.

If you've been asked to serve as the best man, you will set the tone on the wedding day at the reception by offering the first toast. Unless you make your living as a public speaker of some sort, it's important to write out what you plan to say ahead of time. You may have a million and one naughty stories to share from the twenty-odd years you've known the groom, but the reception hall isn't a locker room. Moms, dads, grandparents, and little ones will all be in attendance and looking to you to sum up how special this couple really is. Don't do it by rehashing the night the two of them met in a drunken stupor.

Bachelor and Bachelorette Parties

Okay, so the thought of a bachelor or bachelorette party brings up ideas of debauchery. What it really is is a chance for the soon-to-be-married to have one last "singles" night out with their friends.

> Whether or not to invite someone's parents to a bachelor or bachelorette party depends on the planned activities (though the guest of honor should also have input into the guest list). One compromise, if you'd like to have family involved and then get a little bit wilder, is to have the early part of the day—maybe a game of golf and dinner—include all family members. When dinner ends, the younger crew will head out for a night of drinking and debauchery and the family members will head home.

> If you are a soon-to-be-groom with specific ideas on what you do—or do not—want in a bachelor party, it's perfectly acceptable to let whoever is planning the party know this. If you're the party planner and the guest of honor has made a special request—such as a quiet night in—respect his wishes. You know your friend well enough that he asked you to stand up for him at his wedding, so you should know him well enough to know what activities might be out of his comfort zone. Use your best judgment, regardless of what your own idea of a wild night out may be. **A bachelor party is a "last night" of fun for the groom as a single guy—not the opportunity to humiliate him in front of hundreds of strangers.**

When it comes to the bachelorette party, resolving to stop at three drinks and doing it are two different things once you are surrounded by friends and the night actually arrives. Ask your maid of honor to help you have a great time by discussing the night ahead of time to determine where to set limits. Once the alcohol hits, all bets may be off. If you've already discussed this with your friend ahead of time, you'll know when to take her aside, remind her of her self-imposed limits, and ask how you can help her stick to them. But don't force the issue, or you'll likely be the one who regrets it.

> A bachelor party may be all about celebrating your "last night" as a single guy, but don't take that phrase so literally. Do yourself—and your future wife—a favor and plan the event at least a few days before your actual wedding day (a few weeks is even better). This gives the bride and groom some time to recover from their respective wild nights out and still be able to attend to any last-minute details. And if that night out turned into something scandalous, it also gives the bride enough time to inform everyone that the wedding has been called off.

The Wedding Planner

The bride and groom have final say over who gets invited and whether or not those invited guests can bring a date or their children. This can become a big question mark early on, but the best way to approach it is to speak in absolutes: no kids allowed—not even your favorite nephew—or all kids are invited. **No one wants to leave their uninvited kids with a babysitter, only to show up at a wedding and find twenty-five other tykes tearing up the place.**

> When it comes to allowing singles to bring a guest, many people have adopted the "no ring, no bring" rule, which essentially says that unless a couple is married, single invitees cannot bring a guest. Where this rule is broken is when both parts of a couple are friends of the bride and groom. But speaking in absolutes—and not making exceptions, no matter how desperately someone begs—can keep your conscience clear and make it much easier for you to say no when someone asks about bringing an uninvited guest. Hopefully, it will also prevent them from calling you Bridezilla behind your back.

Just because the titles are gender specific doesn't mean your maid of honor has to be a woman or your best man must be, in fact, a man. Plenty of people choose friends or family members of the opposite sex to play these key roles in a wedding. As long as you're not asking your brother to wear a dress to play the role of maid of honor (also known as an "honor attendant" whereas a female best man is known as a "best woman"), it makes no difference which sex the person is.

The Big Day

Many women grow up dreaming of the perfect wedding day. But there are a number of factors that can, at first glance, seem to ruin that fairy-tale vision.

> Of course, inclement weather isn't the only unexpected "guest" a bride and groom might encounter: a broken leg or severe food poisoning are just two of the unexpected things that have been known to strike a bride or groom on their wedding day. If you've tried every drug and vitamin shot on the market to help you get out of bed and down the aisle and still nothing's working, you'll want to cancel as soon as possible. **If you think you're able to make it through the ceremony and at least a portion of the reception, do your best. But take whatever precautions you can to stay as far away from guests as possible.** For example, you'll want to skip the receiving line so that you don't pass the flu on as a party favor.

> If you're scheduled to attend a wedding and are struck ill or otherwise incapacitated before the big day and don't think that you'll be able to make it, call the bride and groom as soon as possible to alert them to your predicament. They'll appreciate knowing this ahead of time—even if it *is* too late to get a refund on the food.

Gifts for the Happy Couple

You may be hoping for an all-cash-gift affair, but at least one guest is going to arrive with a gift in tow. There should always be a gift table set up that has room for any bags or boxes that someone may have as well as some sort of holder for any cards so that no gift falls on to the floor, blows away, or otherwise goes missing.

> Designate someone in your wedding party—the maid of honor or best man, perhaps—to be in charge of the gifts. When the reception has ended, he or she will be responsible for (carefully) packing all of the gifts away and delivering them to your home (or back to your hotel room). And, no, they can't keep one envelope to cover transportation costs.

CHAPTER 11

Parenthood

First comes love, then comes marriage, then comes [fill-in-the-blank] with the baby carriage. That little ditty that used to haunt us as children is the typical path that life takes. Whether you're going to be a parent for the first time or have scored a reality show deal simply because of the number of kids you've got, the way you behave as a mom or dad dictates who your child will grow up to be.

We're Pregnant!

Discovering that you're pregnant is one of the most exciting times in your life. So it's understandable that you might want to emblazon "We're Expecting!" across every T-shirt you own. But there are right and wrong ways to announce that you've got a bun in the oven to the world at large and generate excitement for Junior's impending arrival.

> It may seem an eternity, but waiting until the end of your first trimester to deliver your big news is the best way to go about it for your own sake. Announcing your pregnancy may be a joyous event—one rife with balloons and fireworks—but as most women who miscarry do so before the twelfth

week of pregnancy, it could be devastating (and an awkward conversation on both ends) to have to explain your miscarriage to the hundreds of people you let in on your previous good news.

> A woman's body goes through a variety of changes when she's with child—nausea, aches and pains, weight gain, and odd cravings being just a few of the more commonly known ones. But many of these very intimate details are best kept between the expectant parents. **Tidbits such as how, where, and when the little one was conceived are no one's business—and fall into the category of TMI for just about anyone.**

No one wants the details of your morning sickness just as you wouldn't want to hear the details of their three-day bout with the flu. Stop and think about whether these are details you would share if your nausea was not pregnancy-related. (TMI is a sometimes side- effect of pregnancy that needs to be closely monitored.)

> One exception to the rule: if your morning sickness has been preventing you from working at your 100 percent best, leaving you in need of frequent restroom breaks, you may want to address this with anyone it impacts—for example, your boss. Better to let him know ahead of time that you may have to rush out of a companywide meeting without time for an excuse.

> On the flip side: when you notice that a coworker has been putting on weight, sneaking an extra donut in the morning, or running out of those very same meetings unexpectedly, don't assume she is pregnant—or ask her when she's due. You know the old saying about those who assume . . .

> A baby's in utero movements are one of the most exciting developments an expectant mother can experience—and often one she wants to share with the world. But not everyone feels comfortable with witnessing the miracle of life with their own two hands. If you feel comfortable letting someone touch your belly and want to invite her to feel the movement, that is fine. **But don't grab your best friend's wrist in the throes of excitement and force her into a discomfort zone.**

Baby Shower

Back in the day, showers—be it bridal or baby—were always a surprise to the guest of honor. Nowadays it's acceptable to keep it a surprise or let the mom-to-be in on the details, and even help with the planning if she wants. Just make sure to let the guests know how clandestine they need to keep things.

> Babies don't come cheap, particularly firstborn children. There are all sorts of high-priced items that all new parents need—e.g., a crib, a stroller—and it is perfectly acceptable for expectant parents to register for these

items. (And it's a great idea for a few shower invitees to get together and opt for one of these items.) But don't go crazy with the high-priced items: this is a baby shower, after all—a time for your friends and family to help prepare you to welcome your baby into the world in comfort and style. This means registering for all the basic essentials such as diapers and onesies and a few of the big-dollar necessities such as a crib and stroller. **Burberry slippers to welcome the new baby home are never considered "necessities."**

> Your feet may be killing you and your entire body may be achy, but even those on bed rest can gather the strength to send out thank-you notes to their guests. Enlist the assistance of a friend at the event to write down each gift and who it is from so you can take a moment to write a proper, heartfelt, and very specific thank-you when the pressure of being the center of attention has passed.

Bringing Home Baby

Finally, the baby has arrived! More and more, mom and baby will be home from the hospital within 24 hours of Junior's birth. This isn't much alone time before the curious—and excited—masses are going to be looking to descend upon you at home to meet your little one.

> If you'd rather have a few days to yourself to adjust to your role as parent and settle the baby into his new home, it's perfectly fine to let others know that. You can even

indicate this as part of the birth announcement: "Mom and baby are doing well, will spend the next several days together, and will reach out when the time is right to have others come over to meet him."

> As a guest to a newborn and new mom, your first visit should always be short. Even if you can't wait to tell the new mom the latest gossip about what's been happening in her absence, this introduction is all about mother and child. So keep your stay short—say hello, admire the baby, give a gift if you've got one, and say goodbye.

> A baby announcement is a great way to let everyone know about your new bundle of joy without having to call every friend or family member directly. If sending a birth announcement, you should do so within two to three weeks of the child's birth and include all of the details that everyone will want to ooh and ahh about: the baby's name; the date and time of birth; height and weight at birth; and hair and eye color. Announcements can be printed on your own computer, professionally printed, or even sent out via e-mail. As many popular names can be used for both boys or girls—Morgan and Jamie, for example—it's nice to choose a gender-specific background color for the announcement (traditional pink for girls, blue for boys) that doesn't leave the recipient guessing whether little Kyle is a he or a she (and what an odd question to have to ask).

Baby Gifts

Unlike with the bridal shower, most people will understand if it takes a new mom a couple of weeks to send a thank-you note for a baby gift. But whether it's three days or three weeks before you put a stamp on that puppy, you must acknowledge each person's generosity and thoughtfulness.

> As in any gift-giving situation, just because someone has given you a gift doesn't mean you need to use it. It's perfectly acceptable to return an item to a store for something that is more appropriate or needed. If you're not sure where the item came from, consider putting it in the closet for an emergency item—or donating it to a local charity. Yes, charity really *does* begin at home.

Baby's Day Out

Eventually, you'll need to emerge from your cocoon of parental bliss and make your way back into the real world, with the little one in tow.

> If you're on your way out and notice that Junior needs to be changed—or fed—do what you can to delay or postpone your appointment. You're never going to get anything accomplished with a wet/tired/hungry infant as your companion. If you weren't able to plan ahead of time—to schedule your appointment so as not to interfere with these vital activities—you need to shift your schedule around to accommodate baby. **It may be 16 years**

until he can get his license, but a newborn is always in the driver's seat when it comes to dictating the day's schedule.

> If you're visiting with friends or family and need help with the baby, make sure that you're not just passing her on to whoever happens to be sitting the closest. Not everyone is a fan of babies—and many people are nervous around infants (in particular, those who have never been parents). Don't just assume that someone will feel comfortable holding your baby without asking permission first. If you sense any sort of trepidation about the prospect of holding the baby while you run out to the car, find an alternate way to get the job done. ("Actually, would you mind running out to the car to grab the baby bag so I don't have to disturb her?") Save yourself one more trip to the car and feel better knowing your baby's in good hands.

If you're the one upon whom the baby is being pushed and you feel uncomfortable holding her for any reason the surest way to get a smitten parent off your back is to let him know that you're just getting over a cold and would prefer not to hold the baby for fear that you may make her sick. Or, if you're a bit on the clumsy side, say so. Chances are, the parent will hightail it in the opposite direction.

> If you're out of the house for more than, oh, thirty minutes, you're likely going to need to deal with a diaper change or two. This is why you packed that bag, remember? You always

want to be fully stocked with baby supplies so that you can attend to the child's needs wherever you may be (she doesn't care if you're in church, at the mall, or anywhere else equally inconvenient). If you're visiting friends or family and need to make a diaper change, ask if there is an outside trash receptacle where you can dispose of the offending bundle. If there is no outside place to stash your trash, wrap it in a plastic bag and leave it in your own car to dispose of yourself once you get home. And maybe stick a neon colored flag on it so you don't forget that it's sitting in the passenger's seat when you get home.

> With their underdeveloped immune systems, children—and infants especially—are particularly susceptible to all sort of germs. In order to protect your child from the bugs that are going around at any given time, you need to insist that whoever holds the baby first gives his hands a thorough washing. You can even make it easy on people by carrying your own bottle of quick-drying hand sanitizer as part of your diaper bag. It may seem like nagging, but anyone who loves babies enough to want to hold your bundle of joy should not be offended when you point the soap in his direction and ask, with a friendly smile, "Would you mind giving your hands a quick wash before holding him? With that bug going around, I want to be extra-cautious." If the person refuses the request, you need to do the same to his request to hold your child.

> We've all encountered the mom who is being dwarfed by her double stroller. While strollers are a godsend for moms

on the go, they can also be a pain to maneuver in tight quarters—both for the person pushing it and for the passersby trying to get around it. Think of a stroller as a moving vehicle, with its own set of safety laws to avoid injuring fellow drivers or pedestrians. Before taking it out on the road, practice pushing the stroller around at home to develop a sense of judgment about how wide, long, and heavy it is. This will make getting in and out of tight spaces a snap—and hopefully accident-free. **Just because you've got that Baby on Board sign hanging from the back of the stroller doesn't mean that people are going to yield.**

> Although it's usually easier for a person to avoid bumping into a stroller than it is for you to see where you're going when wielding one, you need to take responsibility if you hit someone with your stroller. Whether you believe it's your fault or not, apologize and be on your merry way. You don't have time to argue who has the right of way; you've got more diapers to change.

> A crying baby usually indicates one of the following three things: he's tired, he's hungry, or he needs a diaper change. Test out all of these hypotheses and see what you can do to curb the crying. Especially when you're not in your own home, it's important to try and stop the crying as quickly as you can. **If you're tried everything you can think of and still nothing works, no one should be offended if you excuse yourself from the place or event in order to attend to your child at home.** In fact, they will probably be grateful.

Feeding Time

One of the most debated issues in parenting is breastfeeding: some mothers don't even attempt it while others can't imagine any other way. Likewise, while some moms do it just for the first few early weeks, others nurse their babies for a year. Wherever you fall when it comes to breastfeeding, it's important to take other people's feelings into consideration and be courteous about when, where, and with whom you choose to share.

> If you're outside of your home and need to nurse your youngster, try to find a quiet corner in which to do this. The act of nursing a baby can make some people uncomfortable, so it's important to find some sort of semiprivate place in which to do it. Many women's restrooms come equipped with nursing stations and changing areas, making childcare a snap at the mall and other public places—well, as much of a snap as having to change a diaper in a crowded public restroom can be.

> If you are in a location where there are no tucked-away corners, it may be the case that you'll have to feed your baby in the presence of others. Even if there isn't much of an alternative, you should always ask the people you are with if anyone minds if you nurse your baby. If someone is brave enough to admit to you that, yes, he does mind, you need to respect the answer (you did ask the question, after all) enough to try to find an alternate solution—the back seat of your car, maybe? If you must feed your child in a crowd, do your best to give yourself—and the baby—a

little bit of privacy. Draping a blanket over your shoulder while you nurse is one way to give you both a little bit of privacy (so this is another item to keep stored in that trusty diaper bag).

If you need to change your baby in a place where you're not paying the mortgage, you need to ask the homeowners where a good place to do this would be. A kitchen island may save your back from popping out, but is not the best option for the homeowner. If your diaper bag does not come with a diaper-changing pad, buy one on your own and make sure it's always packed away with the rest of your supplies. This is an easy way to turn any surface into a sanitary one for a diaper change, even if the only location is a bathroom floor.

Discipline

Kids learn their behavior from their parents. If little Billy is a little monster, people are going to automatically look at the parents. The line between responsible parenting and clueless parenting is not so thin. **Everyone appreciates a well-behaved tot—even those folks who aren't big kid fans in the first place.**

> Every parent—and even each parent in a couple—has different thoughts on how to discipline his child. In order for your chosen method of discipline to be successful, however, two parents need to be on the same side. Before your

first child is even born, the two of you should look into the future and talk about the ways in which you'll deal with certain situations or possible behavioral problems. If one parent prefers the "ignore it and it will go away" method while the other abides by "address the problem as soon as it occurs" approach, the only thing you'll succeed in teaching your child is total confusion.

> Some parents have a hard time admitting that the way they were disciplined as a child—particularly spanking—is not an appropriate way to discipline a child. Your child may throw such a tantrum that it makes you want to scream, but you're the one who signed on for it. You need to behave as a role model for your child at every turn. **If your child's screaming forces you to scream, what have you really taught him? That screaming begets screaming.**

> Raising your voice to get your point across—and get your child's attention—may be necessary on occasion, but yelling or any sort of physical repercussion is never okay. The phrase "unemotional" should be your mantra when helping to teach a child the proper way to behave. In fact, rather than refer to it as discipline at all—which conjures ideas of spanking—maybe call it just that: "teaching a child the proper behavior." If you feel your blood boiling, take some time to compose yourself to address your child before you say or do something you'll regret.

> A good parent is a conscious parent—one with eyes in the back of her head. Just because your neighbor wants to catch you up on all the latest gossip when you meet up for a playdate doesn't mean you should be so enthralled that you never once turn to check on your child and how he's progressing with his playmates. In fact, your eyes should *always* be on the child—never your gossip-mate—to be sure that he is safe (not trying to climb something or scoot out a door) and getting along well with the other kids (not bopping every kid over the head with his teddy bear as they walk by).

> One thing that is not instinctual: sharing. Human beings, by their very nature, are selfish creatures. The only way a child will learn that not every person, pet, or toy on the planet is at her disposal is for her parents to teach her. It's a particularly important concept for only children to grasp each time they're in the presence of other kids, so use each playdate as an opportunity to help your child further understand that "mine" is not okay. First, though, you need to understand that "sharing" is not a concept that very young children are going to get—no matter how many ways you try and act it out.

> Once a child hits the age of two, you can start teaching the sharing concept by talking about how nice it is to share with friends and show her exactly how she can be a good sharer through role play. Although you should let kids work out any arguments about sharing on their own (their peers will be their best teachers), a kid should

understand that if she and her playmate cannot share a toy, bicycle, etc., then neither of them will be able to use it. This tends to bring out the King Solomon in even the youngest tot. "Taking turns" is an extension of the sharing concept, and is something that should be taught at the same time. (There are many adults who could use a refresher course here, too.)

Eating out is one of a parent's small joys in life, but that experience can go from luxury to tragedy when Junior comes along. It's best to leave very young kids at home with a sitter when enjoying dinner out, or at least to choose a restaurant that is "kid-friendly" so as not to annoy the other couples out trying to have a nice time away from their own kids. You never can predict what will set a young child off—dim lighting, lots of chatter, that horrible Muzak playing over the speaker system.

> If you gave a new parent the choice of teaching their child to be like the well-behaved little one who sits quietly and colors when in a public place and always does what he's told or the little girl who is completely out of control—throwing temper tantrums left and right—which one do you think she'd choose? The good news is that the choice is truly up to the parent, but it's the parents' responsibility to teach the child to behave in the preferred way. Let your child know where it's okay to stretch his

legs and burn off some energy—e.g., the local park—and where it's proper to remain quiet and by mom's side— e.g., a restaurant, the grocery store. If your child is misbehaving or acting in a way that he should not, you need to let him know immediately—and as often as needed. If the child cannot seem to control himself, do the rest of the public a favor and remove him from the situation.

> Practice makes perfect, and that goes for behavior, too. One way to teach your child how to behave in public is to practice at home. If you want to teach a child that dinnertime is not play time—a lesson that can easily translate to a restaurant situation—begin teaching him basic table manners (no talking when your mouth is full, always use your "inside" voice) as early as possible, both by instruction *and* by example.

> Sometimes you need to play the bad guy. Don't let the fact that you're in public dissuade you from disciplining your child. If your child isn't being a good sharer, it's perfectly fine to intervene and "suggest" to your child that he let Suzy take a turn on the slide. If he refuses, it's time for a time-out—or to head home. When a child realizes that by sharing a toy he gets to play with it longer—and by not sharing it he gets to have no fun at all—he'll catch on pretty quickly. That's a smart kid you've got there!

> A shopping trip with your little tyke can be an exercise in refusal. Kids want pretty much everything they see—

whether it's the latest sugar-soaked cereal or the coolest stuffed animal. From one aisle to the next, your child is likely to ask for (or demand) every attractive thing he sees. Do not give in to your child for the sake of silence; this only teaches the lesson that nagging will get you somewhere. (And don't we *all* know an adult or two who surely got *that* message as a youngster?)

> Giving in to a child's every request also makes the special treats you *do* give her less desirable. Instead of giving in to every request, maybe you can identify something she loves—her favorite afternoon snack, her favorite movie— as a "reward" for good behavior. You don't want to set this up as a bribe (though, yeah, that's pretty much what it is) and you don't want to do this with *every* trip to the store or visit to grandma's house. But every once in a while, make a deal with your kid: you behave well and you'll be rewarded accordingly. But any sort of reward scenario needs to be set up in advance—when you're planning the trip—not in the heat of the argument, which then turns this prize into a negotiation. **And when a parent negotiates with his kid, the adult always loses.**

On the Road

When you're traveling, there's often no way to get away from a child's bad behavior—or the fuming of the helpless passengers who are forced to listen to her temper tantrum. But it's not all the kid's fault: traveling takes a lot out of all of us. Whether via car, train, bus, or plane, there are all sorts of annoyances and bad behaviors that can put even the youngest frequent flyer in a bad mood.

> When you're planning a trip with your child, start talking about the trip—and all that it will entail—as soon as possible. Make the travel day seem as exciting as Christmas morning to your child; talk about all the things you'll see and do so that when the big day arrives, your child knows what to expect and is also (hopefully) excited that the day is finally here. He should not be so excited that he doesn't get any shuteye the night before, though, please.

> Distraction is one way to keep your child occupied during a trip—coloring books, video games, movies, books. Whatever toys you can shove into a bag, do. Just make sure that they're quiet toys. If a child has a device on which he can watch a movie, he needs to wear a set of headphones (let him practice with them ahead of time). Bring only those toys that do not create any noise, or that have a mute button. To make the day even more exciting, why not bring a new toy along—something to keep the kid occupied *and* excited.

Swear Jar

Admit it: to hear a young child just learning to say his first words utter a four-letter one is pretty funny. But kids learn their language from somewhere. Unless you're letting them stay up late to watch reruns of *The Sopranos*, anyone who hears this sort of potty mouth is going to suspect it's being learned from you, the parent.

> If your child does repeat a swear word she heard (not from you, of course), while your first reaction may be to laugh, refrain from doing so, at least until you're behind closed doors. **If the child sees that calling Dad an a-hole is the surest way to get a smile out of Mom, guess what name will replace "Daddy" for the next 18 years?**

The best way to ensure that your kid minds his F Yous and F Offs is to refrain from using these sorts of expletives yourself—yes, even when you can find no better way to express yourself. Just imagine that your child is *always* listening. Even when there's a wall separating you. Kids are like sponges: they soak up everything. But unlike a sponge, they release it all later, too, usually in the presence of the last person you'd want to be subjected to a spray of expletives.

> In terms of where you draw the line on what is a "bad" word and what is not, think about the many ways in which a child might be able to use the phrase. Is there a word that's not offensive when used as a noun but grounds for soap in the mouth when used as a verb? Think long and hard about what words you do or do not want your child using. You may agree when Sally tells you she hates Brussels sprouts but what about when she says she hates you? Kids don't have

the ability to distinguish instances in which it's okay and not okay to use sometimes bad words. The best way to make sure they're not used is to eliminate them altogether (from *everyone's* vocabulary).

Tipping for Every Occasion

To tip or not to tip—that is the question. There's often a lot of debate about whether tipping is "required" or not. The fact is that tipping is a customer's way of showing appreciation for a job well done, but in some instances—even if you were unsatisfied with the end result—the solution is to tip less rather than not at all. The real question is: Which service people rely on their tips for income and in which occupations is a gratuity considered a bonus (or incentive, if you will) for a job well done?

Food and Drink

When we think of scenarios where a tip is expected, eating out is probably the first situation that comes to mind. While it used to be the case that 15 to 20 percent was standard, that minimum amount has increased in recent years (call it culinary inflation). Today, an 18 percent tip is the standard minimum for adequate (which is why that's the amount you often see automatically added when you're dining out with five or more people). Speaking of which: before you start carrying the one and moving the decimal point in your head, always make sure the gratuity has not been added for you. This is a practice generally reserved for large parties, but you never know; better safe than 18 percent of your dinner poorer. When you've had a fantastic meal coupled with fantastic service (or even a bad meal coupled with fantastic service), a minimum 20 percent tip is appreciated.

If you've opted for a liquid meal and are only having drinks at the bar, tack on $1 per drink per round for the bartender. If the bar is really crowded and you plan on tying a few on, you may even want to tip heavier on the first round—maybe $5 for your first two drinks—then the standard dollar-per-drink following that; this usually ensures that you won't have to perform any sort of acrobatic tricks in order to get the bartender's attention as the night progresses. (And it can often lead to the bartender buying *you* a round.)

When you want the luxury of a home-cooked meal but don't want to lift a finger to do it, there's always delivery. But what you tip the delivery person can depend on a number of factors, including how much food you've got coming your way and the conditions the delivery person had to go through to get it to you. For orders under $20, tip 20 percent—but never less than $2.00. This holds true even if you're having a $1 cup of coffee delivered. If you're not willing to brew up a cup yourself, you've got to pay someone for the luxury of being lazy.

For orders over $20, a 10 to 15 percent tip is fine, but never give less than $5. And stick to the traditional 20 percent when you've received excellent service. Additional dollars should be given if the delivery person has to trudge through knee-deep snow or pouring rain to get to you or is coming to you during a particularly busy time—the Super Bowl, New Year's Eve, etc.

Beauty Rules
Whether you feel beautiful or not, beauty specialists make a large part of their living from gratuities.

When it comes to hair stylists, for a regular visit—and a great cut—a tip of 15 to 20 percent is standard. If you've deemed someone talented enough to become your regular stylist, always give at least 20 percent to ensure great cuts—and last-minute squeeze-ins—in the future.

To figure out the true cost of a manicure, add in a 15 percent tip every time.

There's probably nothing you wouldn't pay for a great massage. Just make sure you tip the therapist 10 to 20 percent of the total cost.

On the Road

When it comes to travel, there are lots of people you'll meet along the way. And lots who'll be expecting a cash reward of some sort for a job well done.

When someone helps you with your bags, throw them $1 per bag. Add an extra $1 for any extremely oversized or cumbersome packages (as you should have done the time you packed your skis and bowling ball together).

When you arrive at your destination, give the bellman who carries your bags to your room another $1 to $2 per bag.

At the end of your hotel stay, reward the cleaning staff for their hospital corners with a $2 to $3 per-day tip, depending on the size of your room.

Taxi drivers receive a 15 to 20 percent tip on the total fare, plus $1 for every bag they help you with.

A cruise ship is littered with people seeking adventures on the high seas—and employees you'll need to tip, including the stevedore, who carries your luggage and should receive at least $2 per bag. The cabin steward will receive an automatic tip as part of your bill for daily cleaning and nightly turndown service, but you may want to reward a job well done with an extra $25. Likewise, the wait staff will receive an automatic tip as part of your standard service charge, but add at least another $25 at the end of the trip for service well rendered. After looking after your little ones all week so that you could kick butt in shuffleboard, say thanks to the ship's childcare staff with an additional $30 to $50 per kid.

Home Life

Movers: although some say that tipping is not required, have cash on hand and be prepared to tip at least 5 percent. Also: if you've got an extra large move happening, make sure to stock up on cold (nonalcoholic) beverages for the movers and offer to buy them a pizza for lunch if it looks like it's going to be a long day. A well-fed pack of movers will move faster and be a bit more careful with that Picasso.

For the groomer who looks after Fido each week and keeps your furniture fur-free, give 15 percent of each session.

Flowers can be a great surprise—but can also catch you off-guard in terms of tipping. Give the delivery person $2 to $5, depending on what you've got handy.

Holiday Season

When the end of the year rolls around, it's time to show appreciation for all those service people who help you throughout the year, whether you tip them on a regular basis or not. The amount you choose to tip them can vary based on your relationship; if you've never met your postal carrier, you may not feel the need to give him as much as you would the guy you chat with every day.

Child Services

When it comes to your most precious possessions—no, no, your *children*—the end of the year is a great time to show the person who cares for them every day (a nanny or daycare provider) or even part-time (a babysitter or teacher) just how much you appreciate all they've done to help you raise such a fine young man or little lady. Depending on your relationship, and how well she performs in this function, a bonus equal to anywhere from a week's to a month's salary is not out of the question when it comes to nannies and daycare providers, plus a small present from your child. For a regular babysitter, the equivalent of one night's paycheck should suffice along with a small present from your child. Teachers sometimes have a cap on the value of any gifts they can receive, but $25 to $100 is pretty standard. Ask your child if she knows what sort of hobbies that teacher may have—hiking, reading—and buy her something that can be used in that manner, such as a gift certificate to a local sporting goods store. As a payoff for a year of dealing with a room full of kids all day, you can't go wrong with a spa gift certificate, either. For a nonacademic teacher—such as a music teacher or gymnastics coach—a small present from the child equal to $25 or less is a thought that will be appreciated.

Service Men and Women

Sometimes it may feel as if you need to have a pocket of cash and satchel of gifts at the ready at all times during the holiday season, as you'll be tipping and gifting just about every person who does a regular service for you throughout the year—whether you know it or not.

The United States Postal Service does not allow its letter carriers to accept cash tips or gifts valued over $20. So when giving thanks to your letter carrier, keep these rules in mind. Some people choose to give homemade gifts to their postal workers—baked goods, a knitted scarf, etc. But how about the next best thing to cash: a gift card, either in the form of a credit card gift card or to a local business you know your carrier frequents (a restaurant or coffee house where he can rest his cold, dog-nipped feet, perhaps).

Newspaper carriers don't have the same restrictions as postal carriers (lucky for *them*). For daily delivery service, give $25 to $50; for weekend-only deliveries, $10 will keep the good news coming.

If you receive regular deliveries from another mailing service, such as UPS or FedEx, and have a regular driver who delivers your packages, $10 to $25 is appreciated (though not necessarily expected).

If you have a regular house cleaner or maid, throw in an additional $25 for a cleaning close to the holidays.

If you keep your car in a garage, you likely know the regular attendants. Throw each one an extra $10 to $35 apiece when the holidays roll around. Some garages may even provide you with a list of all attendant names (under the guise of a holiday greeting). Yes, you *are* expected to tip them all—not just the one who happens to bring your wheels around as you embark on a holiday road trip. But you can make it easy by, instead of individual tips, leaving one group tip equal to about half your monthly bill. If you have the luxury of being driven around town by a chauffer, 20 percent of a typical month's bill is appreciated around the holidays.

Depending on your relationship with your doorman, whether you tip regularly during the year and how much work he or she actually does for you during the year (those groceries can get heavy, you know), $25 to $75 is an appropriate cash gift. When it comes to the super, again you can adjust by how much interaction you have and what he does for you, but anywhere between $50 and $200 is considered standard (depending on who you ask). If your building employs separate handymen or maintenance workers and/or a gaggle of elevator operators, plan to gift each one with $10 to $50 apiece. Trash collectors receive $20 to $30 apiece.

Luxury Providers

We all have our little luxuries in life—whether it's a dog-walker for Fido or a personal trainer for you, this means that there are even more people to think about come holiday time.

Hair stylists are forever being tipped—but that doesn't mean you should forget them at holiday time. An extra $20 to $100 (depending on the cost of your typical services and how often you go) plus a small token of gratitude (such as a box of chocolates) is good. The same goes for a regular manicurist or anyone else, such as a makeup person, who makes you beautiful on frequent occasions.

When it comes to toning—and relaxing—your body, personal trainers and massage therapists/acupuncturists/body-work specialists should not be forgotten. Give your personal trainer anywhere from $25 to up to one week's worth of workouts and your massage therapist, acupuncturist, or other body-work specialist $50 to $100, or the cost of one session.

You need to throw those folks who look after Fido a couple of bones, too: for a dog walker, that means one to two weeks' pay with a small gift (from the pup). For a regular groomer, it's a small gift plus a cash bonus equal to about a quarter to half of a regular session.

Sentiments for Every Occasion

Sympathies

When someone you know has suffered a loss, let him know with a card that you are thinking about him. This should be sent out as soon as you hear the news. A letter or a store-bought card are equally appropriate here. Just be sure to keep the sentiment short and positive. Never blather on or tell the person you know exactly how they are feeling. Everyone experiences grief in his or her own way; a two-page letter about how you felt when your own father passed away should be saved for your shrink.

Dear Diane:

I was saddened to hear of your mother's passing. I hope that the love and support of your family and friends will help to ease you through this difficult time. You and your family are in my thoughts.

Sincerely,
Jamie

If you knew the deceased well, you should also include a personal memory.

Dear Diane:

I was saddened to hear of your mother's passing. I will always remember how helpful she was when my own mother passed away, delivering a week's worth of dinner to my family. She touched everyone she met with her generosity and will be deeply missed. I hope that the love and support of your family and friends will help to ease you through this difficult time. You and your family are in my thoughts.

Sincerely,
Jamie

Even if some time has passed—you didn't learn about the passing until several months later or simply forgot to send a card—it's never a bad time to let someone know that you're thinking of him and how his loved one touched you or, if you did not know the person, how much you care about the person affected. It's also a great way to remind the person that his loss is still in people's thoughts.

Often in a death notice you'll read that a family has requested donations in lieu of flowers. Respect the family's wishes, even if a call to FTD is much easier. One way that families cope with death as a result of illness is to help find a cure for that illness. If you've opted to make a donation to a charitable organization, do it in the name of the deceased and let the family know that you have done this to let them know you've joined with them in the fight.

If you are the one suffering the loss, even though it may be difficult in the midst of grieving, sympathy cards, flowers, and donations should be acknowledged. Many funeral homes include preprinted cards that you can simply fill out and send. But a handwritten note, expressing your thanks for someone's thoughtfulness during a difficult time, can be a cathartic experience, too.

Dear Jamie:

Thank you for remembering my mother. Your note reminded me of just how much she meant to so many people and helped to ease the pain during this difficult time.

Sincerely,
Diane

In Sickness and in Health

Some people have a hard time dealing with bad news, especially sickness. The easier route seems to be to ignore the situation—and sometimes the person—and pretend it doesn't exist. But can you imagine if the roles were reversed and *you* were on the receiving end of that sort of treatment? Just because someone has learned of an illness doesn't mean that he's living his life in a state of constant gloom and doom. And neither should you. While you don't need to act as if everything is normal, you shouldn't change the way you behave around this person. Let him know that you are there for him and would be happy to help in any way—whether it's driving him to a doctor's appointment or just being an ear to listen to him when he needs it.

Dear Fred:

I was saddened to learn of your recent health problems. Please know that you have my support and love during this trying time—and do not hesitate to call me if you need anything, even if just a chat. My thoughts are with you and your family.

Sincerely,
Tom

Thank You

On a more positive note is the thank-you card—a short and sweet sentiment you'll use to express gratitude when someone has bestowed some act of kindness on you. As with any sentiment, the local card store will have hundreds of cards for just about any occasion—which means you can keep your gratitude short and sweet:

Dear Charlie:

Thank you for dinner the other night. I'm glad I was able to celebrate my new promotion with you—and look forward to returning the gesture soon!

Sincerely,
Vince

Thank-you notes are appropriate on many occasions, such as when you're in receipt of a gift or when someone has done something nice for you—watered your plants while you were away or invited you to lunch to celebrate a promotion.

A thank-you note should be styled generally like this:

Greet the person by name.
Thank him for his act of kindness.
Explain how much this meant to you—and why.
Say thanks again.
Sign your name.

Congratulations!

Engagement, pregnancy, marriage, graduation (not in that order necessarily)—they're all great news and all reasons to send a congratulatory card. While a store-bought card that expresses the sentiment is fine, always add a quick sentence of your own.

Dear Amy:

Congratulations on the newest member of your family. We're looking forward to meeting little Louisa very soon!

Sincerely,
Leslie

Index

About the Author

A former editor for Adams Media, Jennifer M. Wood is the coauthor of the bestselling *Mr. Cheap's New York* and *Mr. Cheap's Chicago* and has contributed to the company's *Everything*, *JobBank*, and *Fast Read* series. Since 2000, she has served as the editor of *MovieMaker* magazine and MovieMaker.com. She is a regular contributor to *Time Out New York*. Jennifer lives in New York City with her husband, Jamie, and their very own Wild Animal Kingdom of pets.